TEEN PATHWAY TO ADULTHOOD

Abraham O. Olayioye

Achievers Publishing Inc
Calgary, Canada

TEEN PATHWAY TO ADULTHOOD

Copyright © 2015 By Abraham O. Olayioye

ISBN: 978-0-9918829-7-7

Published in Canada, by
Achievers Publishing Inc

Canadian Cataloguing in Publication (CIP)
A Record of this Publication is available from the Library and Archives Canada (LAC).

"The right of Abraham Olayioye to be identified as the author of this work has been asserted in accordance with the Copyright, Designs and Patents Act 1988 sections 77 and 78"

For further information or permission, address:
Achievers Consult & Publishing Inc
Calgary, Canada
E-mail: info@achieverspublishinghouse.com
www.achieverspublishing.com

Printed in Canada for Achievers Consult & Publishing Inc

Dedication

This book is dedicated to my father, the I am that I am. The almighty God of heaven and earth for is inspirations and grace in all sufficiency.

On behalf of God, I extend the dedication to my biological Children; Omotolase, Omogbolahan and Omobolaji, my pilot project in youth ministry.

This book is also dedicated to all the Teenagers in Winners Chapel International, Calgary. You shall all transit from Teenage to adulthood without tears in Jesus name.

Acknowledgement

Glory be to the almighty God the giver of life and vision who made this book a reality to bless the on coming generations of the army of Christ.

I acknowledge the person of Pastor Chuka Aguwegbu, whom God used to stir the gift of God in my life for the work of Children evangelism.

I appreciate all my mentors who at one time or the other gave me the privilege to proof myself. May the Lord bless, Apostle David O Ajayi and his wife, Rev Olubunmi Ajayi, Pastor Emmanuel O Ibiwoye and his wife, Pastor Joseph Olumodeji and his beautiful wife.

My sincere acknowledgement to my father, Bishop Joseph Ebohiemen and Pastor Mrs. Christiana Ebohiemen for his spiritual brandishing and mentorship.

If I have seen far into this mission, it is because am sitting on some one's shoulder. I acknowledge the impartation of grace upon my father, Dr. David O. Oyedepo, My Papa and Mama, the Lord strengthen you and cause His face to keep shinning on you.

My sincere acknowledgement to Nick Imoru for his constant support and encouragement to make this book a reality. And to Dcns. Glory Onyeanula and all the Winners Chapel International, Calgary Children department for being a great partner in the current assignment that God committed into our hands. You are all wonderful.

And to my darling wife, Oluwabukolami Esther Olayioye, you are a role model and help meet. Thanks for your support and sincere partnership to help me make a difference in my pursuit.

Table of Contents

Foreword

When Pastor Abraham Olayioye requested my assistance with editing his book, I was both excited and hesitant, not knowing if I was up to the task, and if I would be able to do his work justice. In the last year, I have been transformed from what was a luke-warm Christian to one who feels like I am in the midst of the early church believers, that I have actually graduated from a 'milk to solid food' teaching (I Cor 3:2a), in part by the sound, doctrinal teaching/preaching of Pastor Abraham. Because I have been encouraged as part of the church mandate but mostly by my Lord and Savior and my Father in heaven to be available to serve others, I gladly accepted the task, believing that all such requests have been directed by the God we serve.

Because I have had previous experience as a youth leader, the subject matter was also of great interest to me, and I must admit that not only did I enjoy the challenge of editing this wonderful and pertinent guide for any teen serious about seeking and following the Lord through their teens, but I myself see where I as a parent could have been more supportive, more directional, more emphatic about spiritual training of my children than I was from this book. So, not only is this a powerful resource for teenagers, but I would also recommend any parent of a teen to take the time and effort to read through this guide for successful all-around navigation through the teen years into adulthood. Pastor Abraham addresses all areas of a teen's life, from school, to home, to Church, to friendships, to their walk with God; from where they are in life to the protection and creation of their destiny.

May God bless ALL readers of this book, and may God bless Pastor Abraham with many more years of guiding the youth of WCIC, and many more inspirational writings!

Ruth Yesmaniski-Oghiagbevha
Winners Chapel Int'l
Calgary, Canada

Introduction

Galatians 4:1-7
Now I say, as long as the heir is a child, he does not differ at all from a slave although he is owner of everything, but he is under guardians and managers until the date set by the father. So also we, while we were children, were held in bondage under the elemental things of the world. But when the fullness of the time came, God sent forth His Son, born of a woman, born under the Law, so that He might redeem those who were under the Law, that we might receive the adoption as sons. Because you are sons, God has sent forth the Spirit of His Son into our hearts, crying, "Abba! Father!" Therefore you are no longer a slave, but a son; and if a son, then an heir through God.

"Greatness is not in where we stand, but in what direction we are moving. We must sail sometimes with the wind and sometimes against it." **Oliver Wendell Holmes**

Teenage is a journey that has to be undertaken with caution. Teenage is a 'Passage to Palace'. However, every journey to a palace is assuredly always full of challenges, ranging from oppositions to competitors to sycophants who know well that they are not palace candidates but will not allow anyone to step there for no reasons unknown. It is also a understood fact that no man can enter in to any palace through the back door. As a matter of fact every palace is designed with one entrance. The only royal entrance opens to all royal dignitaries and guests. Any attempt for an alternative route into the palace shall be visited with serious arrest and sanction. No accredited dignitary goes through the back door. Going through the back door into the palace is an offense against royalty, such an offender may be given an everlasting label of 'a generation of violator of the tradition'. His generations yet unborn may also share with him the consequences of such wrong passage. You must be prepared to face all known and unknown challenges to enter into your palace. You have to take responsibility, take care of the oppositions, the competitors and the sycophants that may want to stop you. You have to be responsible for your proper positioning to get there, not by crook but by courage.

Your "youthhood" is your 'useful hood' to take care of your 'future hood', necessary for your settlement in your domain. Your young age is a phase through which you must pass, with the combination of tools and resources, to sail through to your destination in life. It is your most energy-filled phase required to work out your destiny, full of learning points to establish every detail about your destination. It is a receptive stage to take delivery of all necessary instructions, inspiration, counsel and guidance with your openly responsive and highly sensitive mind, a delicate period to pass through hurdles, contentions and challenges against your safe arrival at your destination. Through all of these, there are golden resources available to walk through the path into adulthood.

A teen's life is designed as a Seven Year passage to adulthood. It is a period of seven years of waiting with patience, gathering the truth, observing the direction of the wind, and asking questions for directions and moving towards the next "hood". After this seven years, there is a covenant release. This means freedom. But without been in the covenant, you remain in bondage. Your God's consciousness is the beginning of your covenant walk with God. This is why it is very crucial that you must be born again.

There is a pathway that leads to the palace. It is the pathway of God. This is the golden path to a glorious destination. The "Teenage" phase is a vehicle to your destiny in life. Any mistake on this journey other way outside that of God is the way of doom that may lead to a life of regret for the violator, that may potentially be you, and the generations yet unborn to you. This is why it is very crucial to guide this phase with the greatest care and attention.

Proverbs 14:12
12 There is a way which seemeth right unto a man, but the end thereof are the ways of death.

It is important to understand this terrace and also know the coordinates for easy access and dwelling. The depth of your understanding in this period of your early life will determine where you stand. Where you stand will determine what you see and what you see will determine what you become. Through the teachings and revelation of the Holy Spirit from this book, you are going to receive a place in God to stand and you shall see God, therefore you shall become great in Jesus name.

Chapter 1

Understanding God's Agenda - The Pathway to Glorious Destiny

Jer 1: 5-7 Before I formed thee in the belly I knew thee; and before thou camest forth out of the womb I sanctified thee, and I ordained thee a prophet unto the nations. 6 Then said I, Ah, Lord GOD! behold, I cannot speak: for I am a child. 7 But the Lord said unto me, Say not, I am a child: for thou shalt go to all that I shall send thee, and whatsoever I command thee thou shalt speak.

You have a glorious destiny. You are not a creation of accident. You were God's original concept for a specific purpose. God designed every phase of your life for His glory, He only needs your co-operation to use your life, dedicated to honour Him.

Your presence as a Teenager on this earth at this time in history is preordained. The way you look, the talents and gifts you possess, and the personality you have been given is all part of God's plan. He made you the way you are for a very specific time and purpose, and no one can ever replace you because your purpose of existence is not comparable with another person. You need to be aware of the fact that your 'now' is a preparatory stage for access to your full blown destiny as ordained of God.

But, if you are ever going to fulfil that purpose, your destiny, it begins with believing that you have one and that you must cooperate with God to bring it to pass by adequate preparation into adulthood. Do not be careless with your life. If you do not care about it, no one will or can because you are responsible for whatever becomes of you, not your parents or any other person. What you want to become is in the Bible. Read your Bible, also ask questions, and follow instructions as you are guided by your Pastor, Mother, Father, and Youth Leaders. You have the responsibility to discover your world from the Word of God.

Psalm 139:16 says,
"Thine eyes did see my substance, yet being unperfect; and in thy book all my members were written, which in continuance were fashioned, when as yet there was none of them."

Another Scriptural reference states;

"Before I formed thee in the belly I knew thee; and before thou camest forth out of the womb I sanctified thee, and I ordained thee a prophet unto the nations." *Jeremiah 1:5*

And in Galatians 1:15, the Apostle Paul writes,
"But when it pleased God, who separated me from my mother's womb, and called me by his grace."

I know that many Teenagers never allow the Bible to cross their pathways, nor let it be the basis of what they believe. But these three verses, and there are many more, should be enough to convince you. They are written proof that God knew you even before you were born and that He has a very specific plan for your life that no one else can fulfil. He has a destiny designed just for you but you cannot fulfil it at birth, you must undergo a process of change from Teenager to Adult. There is time for everything,

Eccl 3:1 To every thing there is a season, and a time to every purpose under the heaven:

The word destiny is defined in the America Heritage Dictionary as "the unavoidable or necessary fate to which a particular person is destined. A predetermined course of events." However, I believe that definition is inaccurate. It implies that your destiny cannot be avoided or prevented. This is not scriptural and therefore just not true.

It's true that your destiny is preordained, but it is not unavoidable. Whenever I come across this, it always brings up questions about the sovereignty of God. There are some who teach the sovereignty of God in a way that leads one to believe everything happens for a reason and that God is behind it all.

If this is true, then you have to be prepared to blame God for every evil and 'bad' thing that happens on the earth. That means every catastrophe, every war, every murder, every rape, or any other atrocity you can name must be God's will. If that were true, then God could be said to be a liar. But God forbade evil! He cannot lie nor deny

Himself. God doing evil would be very destructive because it takes away the will to resist evil. Evil **is** avoidable! It is not your portion.

Waywardness is avoidable, you are not designed for it. Pressure is avoidable you have no path with it. Fornication, cheating, lying, laziness are avoidable because they are not part of the redemptive plan of God. You can change anything that is not good about you for good. You have been given the will power to say no. Look at Jabez's case:

1 Chronicles 4:9-10
9 Now Jabez was more honorable than his brothers, and his mother called his name Jabez, saying, "Because I bore him in pain." 10 And Jabez called on the God of Israel saying, "Oh, that You would bless me indeed, and enlarge my territory, that Your hand would be with me, and that You would keep me from evil, that I may not cause pain!" So God granted him what he requested.

You have a right to say "No" to whatever is not a true nature of God nor resembles God in your life. You have a choice to choose what you want, how you want your life to be, you can decide and design your future by choice.

Deu 30:14-16
14 But the word is very nigh unto thee, in thy mouth, and in thy heart, that thou mayest do it.
15 See, I have set before thee this day life and good, and death and evil;

*16 In that I command thee this day to love the Lord thy
God, to walk in his ways, and to keep his commandments
and his statutes and his judgments, that thou mayest live
and multiply: and the Lord thy God shall bless thee in
the land whither thou goest to possess it.*

You are responsible for the choices you make today as it
affects your tomorrow. You need to live with a sense of
destiny ownership. It's important not to go through life
doing your own thing and then asking God to bless it.
The Teenage period is the passage period to perfect the
issue about your destiny.

It is a preparatory period for a stress free, glorious and
enviable destiny. It is a work time to sanitize your
destiny against satanic filthiness. It is time for your full
obedience to God, to your parents and to your teachers,
both scholarly and spiritual. Absolute disobedience at the
Teenage phase of some believing adults today, is the
reason so many believers are experiencing lack of
success, or fulfilment and satisfaction. There is a power
and an anointing that only comes when you are fulfilling
God's plan for your life. And your life starts from your
Teen.

Every person has a pre-ordained plan and purpose for
their lives, but God is not going to make it come to pass
without your concerted effort and responsibility towards
its fulfilment. God will speak to you, and He will woo
you. He wants to reveal His plan for you more than you
want to know it, but it's your responsibility to find out
what it is. Your Teenage is the best platform to secure

the plan and purpose of God so that when you become an adult you are sure of your existence without tears. When you know where you are going, you are sure of it when you get there.

The path way to surety and assurance is the path way of God. As long as you are asking God to reveal His purpose while you are on your way without doing something else, you'll never know difficulty in Teenage and you are sure of easy passage to adulthood.

Though nature and the environment you belong to will pose so many questions to you, don't bother to answer them. Let your answers be from God and to God. He is the right authority over your life and the guide who can guarantee your hurt-free navigation to your tomorrow. Though pressure may come from friends to do things your own way, don't succumb to it. Ask God at every point of pressure what His position is. God has given you all that is needed to move from that position to the destiny He has approved for you, 'an enviable destiny'. You have risen up from the traps of Teenage to the camp of God so that you can have access to ask Him which is the pathway in to your destiny.

Jeremiah 29:13 says,
"And ye shall seek me, and find me, when ye shall search for me with all your heart."

When you finally reach the point where you can no longer live without knowing His will, I guarantee you'll find Him at all times. However, it doesn't happen without your pursuit. Deuteronomy 30:19 makes it very clear that God has given you the power and the freedom to make your own choices. What is your choice?

Deut 30:19 "I call heaven and earth to record this day against you, that I have set before you life and death, blessing and cursing: therefore choose life, that both thou and thy seed may live."

God does not force His will or His plan upon anyone. So, is He sovereign? Yes, if the correct definition for sovereign is utilized. Sovereign means supreme in power or rank. We all would agree with this definition, but I totally disagree with the way religion today uses "sovereign." God does not make His will for our lives come to pass. We have to submit to God and resist the devil (James 4:7). We have responsibility.

Whatever you "will" is what God reigns over. He has given you His alternative as a choice to make. Whatever you chose is what becomes of you. God is the sovereign God by knowing what you don't know, He is kind enough to show you and advises you to make the right choice.

The best example of this is in the Great Commission:
"And he said unto them, Go ye into all the world, and preach the gospel to every creature. He that believeth and is baptized shall be saved; but he that believeth not shall be damned" (Mark 16:15-16).
The Apostle Peter said in 2 Peter 3:9,

"The Lord is not slack concerning his promise, as some men count slackness; but is longsuffering to us-ward, not willing that any should perish, but that all should come to repentance."

This is clear indication that God's intention is not that any man perish, however, whosoever refuses to obey His will as conveyed in His counsel, shall perish. He that believes not shall perish; that is His will.

Scripture cannot be broken without penalty nor be broken without hurt. It's not God's will for people to perish, and yet they do because His will is not automatic. Maybe the person who was called to preach didn't obey, or maybe the one hearing the message rejected it. In either case, God's will did not come to pass. Your destiny will not come to pass automatically either. You have to take your stand to walk in God's pathway into your destiny. The journey of your destiny begins from now as a Teenager.

Whatever God is calling you to do, it is not based on your natural talents and abilities. I am not saying that there is no connection between those natural gifts and God's plan for your life. However, many times God will call a person to do what they seem totally unqualified for. Moses by physical measure as a stammered, was never qualified to lead a crusade of deliverance as a spokesman but God gave him the ability to rise above his disability and he succeeded. God may call you to do the very thing you doubt you are able to. You will know His plan for you by your readiness and early preparation in life.

Your Teenage period is a saving period against the tension of adulthood as the experience of some people. If you would have told me at any point of my teenage phase up till my young adulthood that I was going to be a teacher and preacher of the Word of God, I would have argued it and never in any way gave it a thought. Considering my natural abilities and background, you cannot link me with what I am doing now. This book is a testimony of divine ability against my disability, but I began to think about this as God began to unfold His plan to me and I discovered that everything in my life that I love doing was pointing toward exactly what I am doing now as a Minister of God with the mandate to embark on the reclamation, rehabilitation and enforcing restoration of the glorious destiny of youth from depravity.

God has a destiny for you and I, and He wants to reveal it. But He is not going to chase you down. He is not going to compel you, neither does He force it upon you. That reminds me of Romans 12:1, which says you are to present yourself as a living sacrifice. A living sacrifice is a volunteer. If God were to force your destiny upon you, it wouldn't be a sacrifice; it would be slavery, so, you have to make a choice to follow the pathway of God for glorious and tension free adulthood.

Regardless of any situation you find yourself in today, God is so awesome that He can pardon and relocate you from the wrong place you are, to the right place He planned for you to be. God is like a GPS instrument to the people that are connected to him. When you go the wrong way, He says "Rerouting," and in an instant, He has a new route planned to get you to your destination. It doesn't matter how old you are or what has happened in your past; it's never too late to reroute your way back to the right place. Just believe that you have a victorious destiny, and determine in your heart that you will not take another step in life until you know what it is. Then, just start doing what God is telling you to do.

He won't necessarily give you the entire picture, but He will give you the next step. As you take that step, you will find that there is an automatic anointing that comes to help you accomplish it. It would be unjust for God to call you to do something and then ask you to do it with your own strength and ability.

1 Sam 2:9 *"He will keep the feet of His saints, and the wicked shall be silent in darkness; for by strength shall no man prevail.*

Everything God asks you to do is supernatural. He will always lead you to do something that is beyond your own natural ability so you will have to be dependent on Him. If it's not supernatural then it is natural. The supernatural is superior to the natural. God wants your life to be supernaturally enhanced for tension free Teenage as a cross over path to adulthood. He wants you to be the best!

God's purpose, combined with a willingness to take steps of faith, lead each one into their individual, God-ordained destiny. As you watch, you will sense fulfilment and joy, the kind that only comes when you know you are doing what God created you to do.

Chapter 2

Application of Ten Commandment - Pathway to Regret-Free Adulthood

There is no way you can be victorious without embracing the virtues of the Ten Commandments as a Teenager. The understanding of the Ten Commandments is the surest pathway to victorious teenage passage in to adulthood. You are on the passage to your destiny. Satan, the accuser of man, is hiding at every corner to take undue advantage of your ignorance of the will of God concerning you in order to hinder your victory on the road. The understanding of the terms of your engagement on this road is the determinant factor for your victory. However, you will do yourself a lot of good if you don't only understand it but lay it in your heart during this tender age for greater victory. For effortless assimilation and better understanding, I have endeavoured to creatively sculpt out the Ten Commandments as cited below:

This is a God-inspired order for easy understanding and application of the truth of the Word of God. This was taught to me by one of my mentors as an easy way to remember the Ten Commandments. It is adapted from the KJV:

My Father gave me 10 admonitions against sin for daily application

1."**Thou shalt have no other gods before me**"
This will amount to idolatry, I shall not.

2."**Thou shalt not make unto thee any graven image**"
This is creating alternatives for God, I shall not.

3."**Thou shalt not take the name of the Lord thy God in vain.**"
This is underrating God, I shall not.

4."**Remember the Sabbath day to keep it holy.**"
This is giving God honour due to Him, I shall give it to Him.

5."**Honor thy father and thy mother.**"
This is the way to long life, I shall honour them.

6."Thou shalt not **kill**."
This is the act of destruction of the work of God, I shall not do it.

7."Thou shalt not commit **adultery**"
This is a dirty game before God, I shall not be involved in it.

8."Thou shalt not **steal**"
This is a grievous offence before God, I shall never be involved in it.

9."Thou shalt not bear **false witness against thy neighbour"**

This is an act of wickedness, I shall stay away from it.

10."Thou shalt not **covet"**

This an act of greediness, I shall be good with what I have.

Chapter 3

Attitudinal Prayer Lifestyle - Pathway to Winning Adulthood

Making prayer an attitude is the golden path to the world of triumphant teenager. One of the surest pathway to a teenager's passage to adulthood is the force of prayer. The Teenage period is a forceful period, it takes taking the path of prayer to pass. But you cannot use what you don't have. Therefore, knowing that not many teens know how to pray when they are alone, the following prayer pattern is designed to meet a teen's prayer attitudinal needs.

Sometimes teens have trouble knowing how to pray, particularly if they are alone, so these suggestions are designed to be simple yet powerful for tension free passage in to the world of adult:

Jer 33:1-3
1Moreover the word of the LORD came unto Jeremiah the second time, while he was yet shut up in the court of the prison, saying, 2Thus saith the LORD the maker thereof, the LORD that formed it, to establish it; the LORD is his name; 3Call unto me, and I will answer thee, and shew thee great and mighty things, which thou knowest not..

The following are the prayer format that can form your attitude for endless victory in life.

1. Think and Pray

This is a cool ancient form of prayer that asks you to think back over the last week or month. Let you mind wander through the following questions as you pray:

Thinking back over the recent, past and focus on the moments about the wonders of God in your life. Think on how messy you were and still enjoyed the mercy of God without measure.

In which moments did you give and receive God's love the most even when you least qualified for it.
When were you paying the most attention to the love of God in the world which includes His love for you?

Finish thinking about the personality of God by thanking Him for the gift of today and ask for guidance in being more open to God's presence in your daily life. When you think pray, you suddenly discover all the good things of God in your life and family which results in thanksgiving. It gives you a sense of appreciation because of the understanding of God's abundance for you beyond your present needs.

2. Offer Prayer of Supplication

Matthew Chapter 6
9 After this manner therefore pray ye: Our Father which art in heaven, Hallowed be thy name.10 Thy kingdom come. Thy will be done in earth, as [it is] in heaven.11

*Give us this day our daily bread.12 And forgive us our
debts, as we forgive our debtors.13 And lead us not into
temptation, but deliver us from evil: For thine is the
kingdom, and the power, and the glory, for ever. Amen.*

Using God's word to remind Him of His promises for
you is the act of supplication. Nothing thrills God more
than you putting Him into remembrance with His Word.
Come and let us reason together as requested by God is
not what you do with your head, otherwise you will
misfire, but when you talk according to His Word, He
understands and will do it. Pick up your Bible and start
reading. Select a verse such as "*Truly, I say to you, as
you did it to one of the least of these, my brethren, you
did it to me*" and turn it into a prayer: "God help me to
reach out to the 'least of these' in my world and to treat
them as your beloved children." Or select a psalm as an
inspiration for prayer. Try taking the Lord's prayer
(Matthew 6:9-13) and write your own translation in a
way that reflects your life and needs. Sculpture your
destiny with the scriptures. This is the pathway to a
glorious destination.

3. Pray Quietly
Ps 37:7
*7 Rest in the LORD, and wait patiently for him: fret not
thyself because of him who prospereth in his way,
because of the man who bringeth wicked devices to pass.*
Prayer is two-way communication. If prayer is a
conversation between you and God, then you also need
to listen in silence. Simply sit in silence, perhaps close
your eyes, and see what comes to you.

Meditate on the Word of God and all His wondrous works that are beyond any human's ability. Admire all the good things of God as you meditate on them and ask Him to do His good work in your life. Think more about The Wonders of God, more about their details, their quality, and their texture. Consider what gifts these wonderful things are and give thanks.

4. Give Thanks

Phil 4:6-7 KJV
6 Be careful for nothing; but in everything by prayer and supplication with thanksgiving let your requests be made known unto God. 7And the peace of God, which passeth all understanding, shall keep your hearts and minds through Christ Jesus

Thanksgiving is an essential part of prayer. Any prayer void of thanksgiving is a deformed prayer. That type of prayer cannot go beyond your ceiling. God does not respond to dry prayer such as thankless prayer. The more you think, the more you thank. This is why "Think prayer" is one of the prayer pathways as mentioned in this section. When you are not giving thanks, God considers it as complaining or grumbling. If God must attend to your prayer, it must be routed with thanksgiving. Thank God for yesterday, today and tomorrow. Thank God for what you do not have yet as you thank Him for all that you have. Thanksgiving is the insurance for your possessions. It is the assurance for your tomorrow .No man of thanksgiving lives under tension.

5. Engage in Inquiry Prayer

1 Samuel 30:8. KJV
And David enquired of the LORD, saying, Shall I pursue after this troop? Shall I overtake them? And he answered him, Pursue: for thou shalt surely overtake them, and without fail recover all.

God expects you to make inquiry in prayer. He wants to reason with you and show you reasons for His decisions for you. Ask Him questions that are relevant, not complaining. Make inquiry about what confuses you and let Him clarify to you in detail. What are the big questions of life you require answers for today? Ask, "Why am I here on earth?" "What do you want me to do today?" Spend some time just asking those questions, one after another, offering them to God and see what happens.

6. Use Your Power Of Imagination

Gen 11:4-6 KJV
4 And they said, Go to, let us build us a city and a tower, whose top may reach unto heaven; and let us make us a name, lest we be scattered abroad upon the face of the whole earth. 5 And the LORD came down to see the city and the tower, which the children of men builded. 6 And the LORD said, Behold, the people is one, and they have all one language; and this they begin to do: and now nothing will be restrained from them, which they have imagined to do.

Your imagination is a powerful force for the release of God's power to grant you your desires. Let your imagination be in line with Scripture. Behold in your imagination the power of God as related to all the past acts of God which are recorded in the Bible. You can close your eyes for a while and imagine the world as God would have it be, not as it is, and believe God for a change, asking for it in prayer. What you see determines what you receive from God.

Chapter 4

Happiness - Pathway to a Goodness and Mercy Adult

Happiness is the "state of being happy". This is a concern free, light-hearted, joyful and contented state of being. Happiness is not something that can be defined concretely because it is a relevant state to each individual. It just comes without knowing why, but you are "just feeling it." Salvation is the stimulant of Joy, Joy stimulates happiness. When you have Christ, you have the well of joy inside of you that stimulates happiness and fulfilment beyond you comprehension.

Isaiah 12:3 - Therefore with joy shall ye draw water out of the wells of salvation.

Happiness brings peace even when you are face- to-face with opposition. As a teen that wants to have a peaceful, balanced life, you need happiness. Life does not answer to a "tight face". You have to crave for the joy of salvation. If you are not always happy, then you are not truly born again. One of the evidences of salvation is happiness because you have redemption, a water bearer from the well of salvation. Loosen up, get excited! Be happy and let the devil be mad!

Philippians 4:7 - And the peace of God, which passeth all understanding, shall keep your hearts and minds through Christ Jesus.

How to stay happy

- **Don't be depressed**

Depression is a difficult illness for even the most iron-willed of individuals. Whether you're clinically depressed or just in a rut, depression can make basic tasks like cleaning the house, studying, taking a shower or even getting out of bed incredibly difficult and physically and mentally draining. It is important to stay motivated to continue to live your life, and work towards feeling better, even when you're at your lowest point. Here are some simple ways that you can motivate yourself on a daily basis:

- **Take it easy with yourself**

It's going to take time to get things done in a manner like you used to and to feel like your 'old self'. Changes are not going to happen overnight, so don't be overly critical of yourself if you make mistakes or don't get as much done as you'd like.

- **Be realistic.**

Set up realistic goals and never be too pre-occupied with assignments you cannot finish on schedule. Start with small positive changes and work from there. If you're not realistic you'll just end up frustrated and more depressed.

- **Build around yourself with people.**

Building around you the people that have what you need will be of great help. You need to be around excited people to affect you with excitement! While you may just want to curl up and be alone, this isn't the best or easiest route for you when you're depressed. Having others around you to give you a helping hand, talking to you and providing you with inspiration is important to feeling better and getting back into the swing of things, even if you feel like you just want to shut everyone out.

- **Do not be static**
Lying in bed all day or sitting down and not moving out of a chair is not going to help you; it will only give you more time to feel bad about things. When you force yourself to get up, even if only for a short walk or to attend to some issues outside, you will be helping yourself feel better physically and mentally.

- **Put your hands "on the plough"**
For many, this may seem like that last thing they want to do but an enjoyable project can give you something to concentrate on that will bring your thoughts away from depression and give you something to feel proud of when you're done.

- **Set up a motivating action plan**
If even the smallest tasks seem like a chore, start small with planning out what you're going to do each day. In the morning, write down the things you'd like to accomplish and in the evening, go back and check off what you did. This can help you regain your sense of control over your life at a time when it seems the most depressing.

Recovering from depression is a hard road, but with some planning and slow but steady progress you will be able to start feeling optimistic about your life again. Your case is never closed before Jesus. You can't be around Him and be depressed. I curse all traces of depression in your life today in Jesus name.

- **Get involved in a Teens group**

Your involvement in a Teens activity group is an antidote against depression. You are depressed because you are not functioning as God intended. Join a Teen prayer group, a Teens Choir, a Teens Bible study group or a Teens care group to get busy and functioning. When you are functioning in the hands of God, you become an oppression. Nothing can depress you when you are always in the presence of God. I release you into the realms of joy unspeakable from now, in Jesus name.

Chapter 5

Understanding your Personal Creativity - Pathway for Profiting

I used to wonder at myself, how I come up with creative ideas when nobody thought me to be a creative person. I actually have great motivation for creativity. I came to the conclusion that all of us are born creative. We are born with a "Sense of Wonder". We are all born with innate ability, potentials that can never be exhausted if well utilized for our advantage and to the glory of God. But many of us, as we get older we tend to lose our sense of wonder and creative ability. We forget how to "think outside the box" and tend to see things in only one way. But give a child a banana and it becomes more than a healthy snack. With a little imagination it becomes a gun, a smile or a frown, a mobile phone, a nose, an antenna, a flute, and even more. As a Teen that wants to make a difference, you have to realise you have a potential crying for expression. You also have the responsibility of giving your potential or if you prefer to call it talent, the right attention for it to find expression.

How can I regain my creativity is the first question of curiosity that you need to ask. What is the solution for rediscovering your talent is another intelligent question you have to start asking. The following will help you rediscover or redefine your potentials.

1. Free yourself from limitations

Attempt the impossible. Think the unthinkable and you will experience the unimaginable. Break out of the walls, take on the qualities of a rubber band - be flexible. Embrace the ridiculous and challenge the rules. What if the impossible were possible. You have all it takes, just take a step and see your creativity at work.

2. See things around you beyond what they are

a. Think possibility against all odds. Change the perspective of things in your thinking to achieve the unimaginable. Let your thinking be, "What if the cat was the elephant or the elephant the cat?" "What if the ice was hot and the fire was cold." "What if the snail was fast and the bird too slow."

b. Take things to extremes and beyond the normal. Imagine the ridiculous, exaggerate a quality or characteristic and expect the unexpected.

c. Think "otherwise". What if you were teaching race-car driving to the golf pro. Or golf to the race-car driver. What if you were giving the lesson at the beach, in a cave, in the morgue, on the moon? What if you were teaching in the kitchen, the toy store, on the farm, in the blacksmith shop. What if you suddenly became another Jesus by God's choice. Just think "outside the box" for effect. Think revolution and expect it where you want it to happen through you.

All these things change your perspective. Some of the world's greatest inventions and achievements came from people looking at things from a different perspective.

3. Get inspired with everything around you.

The Bible, Leaves, Chemistry, School Supplies, Nature, Household items, a Butterfly, Machines, Lions, Science, the Body, Shapes, Colours, Textures, Street lights, News magazines, , Movies, Cartoons, Occupations, Songs, Hobbies, Books, Clothes, Famous personalities, Flavours, etc.

a. Look to your senses - How would you describe things according to smell, to touch, by sound, taste or sight?
b. Look around you - Walk through a toy store or any other store, empty your junk drawer, visit an appliance store, a supermarket or a bakery. A Christmas tree, what if it were a bird, an animal, an insect, a fish?
c. Look to others - The most creative people in the world are those who draw intelligently from the idea "well" of others.
d. Look for similarities, differences, and various characteristics. What objects, things have similar attributes?

4. Look Inward and Outward

Imagine how God does all that He did and think of how you can do like He did to glorify His name. Think about the Creator and the Creation and you as one, ready to recreate.

5. Consider your past

How did things go with you when you used to do some creative things as a child? What makes things work the way they worked then, and how can you resurface the advantage to bring your creativity back to life. What inspirations came to mind as you continue to look back at your productive ability with amazing creativity?

6. See in to your future

How could it be done better next time? Write it on a card and place it in a file for future use. You are a creature of unlimited possibility. All that makes things possible are in you. You can make things happen, because you are loaded with the creative ability and power of God. You are essentially a Teenager ready to turn your world upside down with witty inventions. You shall not be a misfit to your generation in your own time. Your skill developed is the guarantee for your shining.

Chapter 6
Skills Development - Pathway to Reign in Adulthood

Gen 14:14
14 And when Abram heard that his brother was taken captive, he armed his trained servants, born in his own house, three hundred and eighteen, and pursued them unto Dan.

You have to identify your skill; develop your capacity. Sharpen your soft skills and endeavor to master many skills as soon as possible. Your age is not in any way a barrier. You are not too young to be skilful. Teenage is an age of training. The Youth phase is the "useful phase". All of us have a certain skill set, often based on our jobs, our high school training and extra- curricular activities, current and past, our hobbies and our day-to-day experiences. Employers tend to be interested primarily in skills – what you can do. Some of these will be very specific to particular jobs, technical skills, such as being able to program a computer and other skills which are "transferable skills" that you can use in many careers as well as in day-to-day life, such as public speaking or presentational skills, sport and athletics.

Think deeply and examine yours skill advantage. Sit down and list your skills, identify them to enable you to know which one needs upgrade. Identify what skills you can develop, with the investment of a little time and money. Some ways to invest in your skills are:

a) Read a book that teaches you something new in a particular area of your interest or possessed skill.
b) Attend seminars, workshops and any capacity development programs.
c) Take part in an online professional courses that can enhance your skill.
d) Ask someone to mentor you in your identified skill and anticipated career.
e) Schedule a regular time to practise your skill, do not allow it to become obsolete.

Chapter 7

Maintenance of Good Health - Pathway to a Healthy Adulthood

3 John 1:2
2 Beloved, I wish above all things that thou mayest prosper and be in health, even as thy soul prospereth.

God's will for you is sound, healthy living. You don't live healthy by wishing. You live a healthy lifestyle by conscious effort towards healthy living through what you eat, drink, wear and use.

Teens, for many reasons, create ill-health situation for themselves due to careless and riotous living. Too many of us are storing up health problems for later life, ones that could cause financial problems or give us a huge reduction in quality of life. What you eat, what you drink and what you wear have a way of affecting your health. You have to give your health the necessary care and attention today to have a healthy tomorrow. It's much cheaper to focus on staying healthy than to take preventative action once something has gone wrong. If you're in good health, your performance will be better at school and at work. You will have more energy to work towards your goals, and you will generally feel happier.
You must give attention to both your physical health and mental health, they are both important. Your mental and

physical health cannot be considered complete in isolation of one another. By investing some time and little money from your savings and parents budget now, you could save yourself a huge amount of both in the future. Here are some ideas to get you started:

1. Ensure you use a screen protector with your computer to maintain good eyesight.
2. Visit dieticians for a proper diet outline if you are the type that does not feel good about the quality of food you are eating.
3. Eat a good and healthy, balanced diet, feed on fruits, veggies, whole grains and lean proteins.
4. Avoid smoking, drugs and alcoholic drinks.
5. Watch and manage your over or under weight through scheduled exercise.
6. Do helpful exercises every day for maintenance of your heart and to refresh your mind and brain.
7. Maintain good dental hygiene and visit your dentist for check-ups.

Consider the ways in which you can remain healthy and keep working on it. Do not just eat anything, eat what is profitable to your health. Exercise your body and never allow it to become stagnant.

Chapter 8

Personal Caution - Pathway to a Secured Adulthood

Personal caution will give you peaceful living that nobody can contest. The more careful you are, the more glorious crown you wear. Your sense of caution is the determinant factor for your safety. When you mind the covenant of God with a reference to the Ten Commandments and God's wise counsel, you will be at peace. Out of multitudes of counsel, there is safety. What you do with counsel is to arm yourself with caution. You cannot be a victim of Satan if you do not have relationship with him. He only accuses you based on your interplay with him. Caution is the key to safety.

The following are the Caution keys required for success. They guarantee safety any time you bring them to bear in your life. The Teen phase is the toughest phase so you need a lot of caution to sail through it.

1. Caution Key of Satisfaction
Being comfortable with whatever you have or has been made available to you for the time-being, be it material things or endowments from God.

2. Caution Key of not being Over- Ambitious
The dedication to a cause greater than oneself, with little or no selfish motives, is the greatest enabler of success. Some body said, "In other words, not caring

about success will sooner provide a higher quality of success than a hyper-intentional desire to quickly create it".

3. Caution Key of Knowing Who You Are

Know who you are and don't allow it to go to your head. The simple awareness of who you are, where you are going and why you are going is the security against confusion in life. This is so that everywhere will not look like where you are going, thereby creating tension and anxiety.

4. Caution Key of Humility

There is power in 'HUMILITY' and assuming the 'low position'. Rivers flow to the ocean because it is in the lowest position; the high declines toward the low; a ship floats because the hull is hollow; simplicity is stronger than complexity; less is more; creation follows destruction; something comes from nothing; and somebody comes from nobody. God resists the proud but gives grace to the humble. Pride leads to destruction.

Chapter 9

Personal Development - Pathway to Connecting to Adulthood

One great question to ask if you're interested in self-improvement is "Am I investing in myself?" particularly when you're feeling stuck, or when your progress towards your goals hasn't been as fast as you'd like. So what does "investing in yourself" mean? This depends on what your goals are, but these are three big areas you might want to invest some time, money and thought in:

- Your skills (discussed in Chapter 6)
- Your health (discussed in Chapter 7)
- Your appearance

All of these are important for success in all walks of life. The last of these investments is your appearance.

Investing In Your Appearance
This might seem a very shallow thing to write about, but unfortunately, like it or not, we all tend to judge on appearances. In some jobs or roles, looking the part can make a real difference to how others perceive and treat you.

Just as importantly, your appearance can have a huge effect on your self -confidence. Have you ever been at an event where you misjudged the formality and ended up very under-dressed or over-dressed. If so, I am positive you felt awkward and out of place. In the same manner, you might well have taken extra care over your grooming before a big presentation and felt more confident as a result. Investing in your appearance might mean:

- For young men, saving up for a good suit, shirts and matching pants, for young ladies non-exposing blouses, sweaters, skirts and dresses of modest length, non-skin-tight slacks and jeans; and tasteful use of makeup
- Asking a fashionable friend for advice on your usual "look"
- Losing some weight.
- Taking some time to change and reorganize your wardrobe, ensuring you have clothes that mix and match well

Chapter 10

Good Relationships - Pathway to a Responsible Adulthood

Relationship is vital. John Donne spoke truth philosophically when he wrote "No man is an island entire of itself". Relationship is what leads to being reliable. Without it you have no remarks. If you want to enable a speedy success, you need to be connected to people. Good relationship is the key to enviable destiny void of tension.

Healthy relationships should be built on a degree of detachment. Here, people often make a mistake; they think that being detached means, "not caring". However, this is not the case. Often when we develop a very strong attachment, we expect the person to behave in a certain way. When they don't, we feel miserable and try to change them. A good friendship based on detachment means we will always offer good will, but we will not be upset if they wish to go a different way.

The way you comport yourself and talk will determine who relates with you. People need honest people to relate with. You need to be of good manner to matter in relationship. Mind the way you talk and be wise in dealing with people.

Below are some valuable nuggets to maintain a healthy relationship that enhances your destiny to reach it's limelight in life.

1. Talk less and listen more
Most people get tremendous pleasure from speaking about themselves but here we have to be careful; if we always speak about our achievements or tribulations, people will get fed up with what stems down to our pride. One wise man said "Speak a little less, listen a little more."

If we are willing and able to listen to others, we will find it much appreciated by our friends. Some people are not aware of how much they dominate the conversation.

If you are the type that is always talking, talking about yourself, consider the advice of the Greek philosopher, Epictetus: "Nature gave us one tongue and two ears so we could hear twice as much as we speak."

2. Embrace a win –win life style
A lot of problems in relationships occur because we want to maintain our personal pride, whether we identify it as such or not. Don't insist on always having the last word. Healthy relationships are not built through winning meaningless arguments. Be willing to back down; most arguments are not of critical importance anyway.

3. Avoid gossip
If we value someone's friendship we will not take pleasure in commenting on their frequent failings to

others. Inevitably, they will eventually hear about it but whether we get found out or not, we weaken our relationships when we dwell on negative qualities. Avoid gossiping about anybody; subconsciously we don't trust people who have a reputation for gossip. We instinctively trust and value people who don't feel the need to criticize others.

4. Forgiveness

Forgiveness is not just a gospel truth, it's a powerful and important factor in maintaining healthy relationships. However, real forgiveness also means that we are willing to forget the experience. If we forgive one day, but then a few weeks later bring up the old misdeed, this is not real forgiveness. When we make mistakes, just consider how much we would appreciate others forgiving and forgetting.

5. Silence is golden

If you think a friend has a bad or unworkable idea, don't always argue against it; just keep silent and let them work things out for themselves. It's a mistake to always feel responsible for their actions. You can offer support to friends, but you can't live their life for them.

6. Be guided with good intention

If you view friendship from the perspective of "What can I get from this?" you are making a big mistake. This kind of relationship proves very tentative. If you make friendships with the hope of some benefit, you will find that people will have a similar attitude toward you. This kind of friendship leads to insecurity and jealousy.

Furthermore, these fair weather friends will most likely disappear just when you need them most. Don't look upon friends with the perspective "What can I get out of this?". True friendship should be based on mutual support and good will, irrespective of any personal gain.

7. Be humorous

Don't take yourself too seriously. Be willing to laugh at yourself, even to be a little self-deprecating. This does not mean we have to humiliate ourselves, far from it, it just means we let go of our ego. Humour is often the best antidote for relieving tense situations.

8. Develop healthy relationships

Maintaining healthy relationships doesn't mean we have to spend several hours in the home of friends when you have no meaningful things to do. It means we take a little time to consider others, remembering birthdays and anniversaries etc. But, it is a mistake to spend several hours ruminating and dissecting relationships. Good friendships should be built on spontaneity and newness, sharing a moment of humour can often be of more benefit than several hours of discussion.

Chapter 11

Positive Action Habit - Pathway to Exploits into Adulthood

People at the top of every profession share one quality — they get things done. This ability supersedes intelligence, talent, and connections in determining the size of your salary and the speed of your advancement.

Despite the simplicity of this concept there is a perpetual shortage of people who excel at getting results. The action habit — the habit of putting ideas into action now — is essential to getting things done. Here are 7 ways you can grow the action habit:

1. Don't wait until conditions are perfect – If you're waiting to start until conditions are perfect, you probably never will. There will always be something that isn't quite right. Either the timing is off, the market is down, or there's too much competition. In the real world there is no perfect time to start. You have to take action and deal with problems as they arise. The best time to start was last year. The second best time is right now.

2. Be a doer - Practice doing things rather than thinking about them. Do you want to start exercising? Do you have a great idea to pitch to your boss? Do it today. The longer an idea sits in your head without being acted on, the weaker it becomes. After a few days the details gets hazy. After a week it's forgotten completely. By becoming a doer you'll get more done and stimulate new ideas in the process.

3. Remember that ideas alone don't bring success – Ideas are important, but they're only valuable after they've been implemented. One average idea that's been put into action is more valuable than a dozen brilliant ideas that you're saving for 'some other day' or the 'right opportunity'. If you have an idea that you really believe in, do something about it. Unless you take action it will never go anywhere.

4. Use action to cure fear – Have you ever noticed that the most difficult part of public speaking is waiting for your turn to speak? Even professional speakers and actors experience pre-performance anxiety. Once they get started the fear disappears. Action is the best cure for fear. The most difficult time to take action is the very first time. After the ball is rolling, you'll build confidence and things will keep getting easier. Kill fear by taking action and build on that confidence.

5. Start your creative engine determinately – One of the biggest misconceptions about creative work is that it can only be done when inspiration strikes. If you wait for inspiration to slap you in the face, your work sessions will be few and far between. Instead of waiting, start your creative motor by resolution to do so. If you need to write something, force yourself to sit down and write. Put pen to paper. Brainstorm. Doodle. By moving your hands you'll stimulate the flow of ideas and inspire yourself.

6. Live in the present - Focus on what you can do in the present moment. Don't worry about what you should have done last week or what you might be able to do tomorrow. The only time you can affect is the present. If you speculate too much about the past or the future you won't get anything done. Tomorrow or next week frequently turns into never.

7. Get down to business immediately – It's common practice for people to socialize and make small talk at the beginning of meetings. The same is true for individual workers. How often do you check email or RSS feeds before doing any real work? These distractions will cost you serious time if you don't bypass them and get down to business immediately. By becoming someone who gets to the point you'll be more productive and people will look to you as a leader.

It takes courage to take action without instructions from the person in charge. Perhaps that's why initiative is a rare quality that's coveted by managers and executives everywhere. Seize the initiative. When you have a good idea, start implementing it without being told. Once people see you're serious about getting things done they'll want to join in. The people at the top don't have anyone telling them what to do. If you want to join them, you should get used to acting independently.

Chapter 12

Understand Your Own Intelligence - Pathway to Industrious Adulthood

Many years ago I listened to a lecture on cognition that changed the way I think about intelligence. This is the crux. There are two types of cognition. The first is normal cognition. This is the ability to retrieve knowledge from memory. When you are asked a question on a test and produce an answer, that's a display of cognitive ability. The second type of cognition is metacognition; the ability to know whether or not you know.

Have you ever been asked a question that you knew the answer to, but you couldn't find the right words. This is called the 'tip of the tongue' phenomenon and I'm sure we've all experienced it. You know that you know the answer, but you fail to produce it. If someone told you the answer, you would know instantly, whether it was correct or not. In these cases metacognition exists without cognition. In short, cognition is knowing, metacognition is knowing if you know or not. Both can exist together, but many times they don't.

How Does this Affect Your Intelligence?
Of what importance is this and how is it relevant to self-improvement? The fact that there are two different kinds

of cognitive ability means that there are different types of intelligence.

In conventional education, intelligence is measured by cognitive ability. For some people this works well. They can easily produce everything they know on a test. But for others it doesn't work out so well. The people that know something with certainty but can't find the right words on a test are awarded with poor grades and considered inferior.

Does this inability make them any less intelligent? They know the answer. If the question came up on a task, they could refer to a book or a quick Google search. In reality they're just as effective as the people that attempted the test and were successful in answering all the questions. They just can't prove it as easily.

The Importance of Knowing What You Know
Unless you're taking a test or playing games, metacognition is more important to success than cognition. In real life, when you're faced with a question, the first decision is whether you know the answer or not. With strong metacognitive ability this is easy. If you know the answer, but can't come up with it, you can always do a bit of research. If you know for sure that you don't know, then you can start educating yourself. Because you're aware of your ignorance, you don't act with foolish confidence. The person who thinks they know something that they really don't makes the worst decisions.

A person with poor cognitive ability, but great metacognitive ability is actually in great shape. They might do poorly in school, but when faced with a challenge, they understand their abilities and take the best course of action. These people might not seem intelligent at first glance, but because they know what they know, they make better decisions and learn the most important things.

Clever but Mediocre People
At the opposite end of the spectrum are people with great cognitive ability but poor metacognitive ability. These people are proclaimed geniuses at a young age for "ace-ing" every test and getting great SAT scores. Unfortunately, they've been ruined by poor metacognition; they think they know everything but they really don't. They are usally arrogant, fail to learn from mistakes, and don't understand the nuances of personal relationships; showing disdain for persons with lower cognitive ability.

In a battle of wits the higher cognitive ability prevails, but life is not a single encounter. It is a series of experiments in succession, each building upon the last. Learning requires a knowing of what you don't know, and taking steps to learn what you need to. People with poor metacognitive ability never realize that they don't 'get it'. They also don't realize what's important.

This doesn't preclude them from material success but perhaps that's a poor measurement of intelligence as well. There are many people who become rich and successful by their cleverness and cognitive ability, but as caring human beings are quite mediocre. Is the man that makes a million dollars but is cruel and abusive to his employees and family really more intelligent than the poor man who lives a modest and loving life? I don't intend to demonize wealth, only to state that it should not be the measure of virtue.

Use Your Metacognitive Ability

So what do we know and what do we not? And how can we tell the difference? There is so much to know in the world that the most brilliant human minds can grasp only the tiniest fraction. For this reason we should always be in doubt of what we know. The closed mind is oblivious to its surroundings, while the open mind absorbs it. Like a sponge, it soaks up all observations, becoming fuller and more robust.

We can't live in total doubt. If we did we would never act, paralyzed by our inadequate knowledge. We must trust our intuition. If something makes you feel a certain way, that feeling is real and must be respected. Act based on your own convictions, not those of others, and keep an open ear for new ideas.

The most important mental power is the ability to know what you don't know. The recognition of a fault is the first step to improvement. Don't try to hide a lack of knowledge. People will see through it and you'll appear foolish and arrogant. If you admit your ignorance, people will help you learn and also respect your humility. For intelligent people this is the toughest lesson to learn. We are used to being right, and consider being wrong shameful. We're afraid to lose status by looking stupid. This vain arrogance is a great weakness and the source of many problems. To crush it and embrace humility is the mark of true wisdom.

Chapter 13

Sound Bible-based Decision Making Steps - Pathway to Error-free Adulthood

Begin with prayer. Frame your attitude into one of trust and obedience as you commit the decision to prayer. There's no reason to be fearful in decision making when you are secure in the knowledge that God has your best interest in mind.

Jeremiah 29:11
"For I know the plans I have for you," declares the LORD, "plans to prosper you and not to harm you, plans to give you hope and a future." (NIV)

Define the decision. Ask yourself if the decision involves a moral or non-moral issue. It is actually a little easier to discern the will of God in moral areas because most of the time you will find clear direction in God's Word. If God has already revealed his will in Scripture, your only response is to obey. Non-moral areas still require the application of biblical principles, however, sometimes the direction is harder to distinguish.

Psalm 119:105
Your word is a lamp to my feet and a light for my path. (NIV)

1. Be ready to accept and obey God's answer. It's unlikely that God will reveal his plan if He knows already that you won't obey. It is absolutely essential that your will be completely submitted to God's. When your will is humbly and fully submitted to the Master, you can have confidence that He will illuminate your path.

Proverbs 3:5-6
Trust in the Lord with all your heart; do not depend on your own understanding. Seek his will in all you do, and he will show you which path to take. NLT

2. Exercise faith. Remember too, that decision making is a process that takes time. You may have to resubmit your will over and over again to God throughout the process. Then by faith, which pleases God, trust him with a confident heart that he will reveal his will.

Hebrews 11:6
And without faith it is impossible to please God, because anyone who comes to him must believe that he exists and that he rewards those who earnestly seek him. NIV

3. Seek concrete direction. Begin investigating, evaluating and gathering information. Find out WHAT THE BIBLE SAYS about the situation. Gain practical and personal information that relates to the decision, and begin writing down what you learn.

4. Obtain counsel. In difficult decisions it's wise to get spiritual and practical counsel from the godly leaders in your life. A pastor, elder, parent, or simply a mature believer can often contribute important insight, answer questions, remove doubts and confirm inclinations. Make sure to choose individuals who will offer sound biblical advice and not just say what you want to hear.

Proverbs 15:22
Plans fail for lack of counsel, but with many advisers they succeed. NIV

5. Make a list. First write down the priorities you believe God would have in your situation. These are not the things that are important to you, but rather the things that are most important to God in this decision. Will the outcome of your decision draw you closer to God? Will it glorify Him in your life? How will it impact those around you?

6. Weigh the decision. Make a list of the pros and cons connected with the decision. You may find that something on your list clearly violates the revealed will of God in his Word. If so, you have your answer. This is not His will. If not, then you now have a realistic picture of your options to help you make a responsible decision.

7. Choose your spiritual priorities. By this time you should have enough information to establish your spiritual priorities as they relate to the decision. Ask yourself which decision best satisfies those priorities? If more than one option will fulfil your established priorities, then choose the one which is your strongest desire!

Sometimes God gives you a choice. In this case there is no right and wrong decision, but rather a freedom from God to choose, based on your preferences. Both options are within God's perfect will for your life and both will lead to the fulfilment of God's purpose for your life.

8. Act on your decision. If you have arrived at your decision with the sincere intention of pleasing the heart of God, incorporating biblical principles and wise counsel, you can proceed with confidence knowing that God will work out His purposes through your decision.

Romans 8:28
And we know that in all things God works for the good of those who love him, who have been called according to his purpose. (NIV)

Chapter 14

Imbibe Godly Character - Pathway to Honourable Adulthood

2 Peter 1:5-11

5 But also for this very reason, giving all diligence, add to your faith virtue, to virtue knowledge, 6 to knowledge self-control, to self-control perseverance, to perseverance godliness, 7 to godliness brotherly kindness, and to brotherly kindness love. 8 For if these things are yours and abound, you will be neither barren nor unfruitful in the knowledge of our Lord Jesus Christ. 9 For he who lacks these things is short-sighted, even to blindness, and has forgotten that he was cleansed from his old sins.10 Therefore, brethren, be even more diligent to make your call and election sure, for if you do these things you will never stumble; 11 for so an entrance will be supplied to you abundantly into the everlasting kingdom of our Lord and Savior, Jesus Christ

This was a holy charge from the apostle Peter about the Godly-look requirement of a Teenager that guarantees tension free life. Your Godly- character trait is all you need for a colourful destiny. You have to look like God to enjoy the comfort of God. Any life void of God's character will soon crash. You can live an accident-free life by imbibing God's kind of character. You are hereby admonished to pursue after Godliness for by it you have great gain. The responsibility required from you is to seek after and pray for the likeness of God's nature to enjoy the mercy of God.

Nothing can be more rewarding, satisfying, and fulfilling as knowing Christ and living in the freedom of obedience to Him. It becomes easy to live like God when you possess the character of God.

1. **Be a God-Centered Teen**

A God-centered person is a person without an alternative to God. He is a person that is lost in the will of God. Show me a person who is sold out to God; he is the person that feels the most comfortable with Him in all things. He gives thanks whether things are yet working as expected or not, he has dedicated his life to glorify Him at all times. He or She is a man or woman whose thoughts and actions are guided by God. You were made by God to be God-centered. Praise and glorify God by how you live, how you study, how you play, how you converse, and how you relate.

2. Be a Teen of Faith

Hebrews 11:1-3 KJV

11 Now faith is the substance of things hoped for, the evidence of things not seen.2 For by it the elders obtained a good report.3 Through faith we understand that the worlds were framed by the word of God, so that things which are seen were not made of things which do appear.

Faith is the language that God understands for you to be able to receive from Him. Faith is the state of absolute dependence on God. It is a spiritual communication that compels God to act in your favour. Faith is the spiritual responsibility required of you to obtain what you need from God. It is the price you pay to attain the higher heights in life. It is a spiritual force that provokes heaven to open over your head for landmark experience.

Your faith should not be just one part of your life. Instead, it should guide, direct, permeate, and inform every area of your life at home, at school, in the car, with your friends, on the athletic field, etc.

3. Be a 'Thanksgiver' Teen
1 Thes 5:18 KJV
18 In every thing give thanks: for this is the will of God in Christ Jesus concerning you.

Everything you have, are, and do is a gift from God. Don't think they come from you. Instead, realize that all the good gifts you experience are purely by the grace of God. And when you experience emotional, spiritual, or physical challenges be especially sure to thank God for them as gifts. He's given you those challenges as part of the refining process for your greatness, not for tension. He's growing your faith as you are growing so that you don't groan in life. Thankfully recognize the source of your blessings and give the relevant appreciation.

4. Be a Teen of Accurate Discernment
1Cor 2:14

14But the natural man receiveth not the things of the Spirit of God: for they are foolishness unto him: neither can he know them, because they are spiritually discerned.

Your life will be full of choices. Many of them difficult choices that require clear direction. The level of attention you receive in life is determined by the quality of direction you receive from God. Let your choices be tailored to what you discern spiritually from God. Ensure that all your decisions, what you listen to, what you watch, who you choose as close friends, who you marry, how you spend your time, what you do vocationally is on the basis of God's unchanging Word that gives you accurate discernment to choose or make right decision. Don't trust your changing feelings as a gauge to discover and do what seems right. Instead, study and follow God's Word so that you can choose to do what is right.

5. **Be a Teen of Grace**
2 Corinthians 12:9-12 KJV
9 And he said unto me, My grace is sufficient for thee: for my strength is made perfect in weakness. Most gladly therefore will I rather glory in my infirmities, that the power of Christ may rest upon me. 10 Therefore I take pleasure in infirmities, in reproaches, in necessities, in persecutions, in distresses for Christ's sake: for when I am weak, then am I strong. 11 I am become a fool in glorying; ye have compelled me: for I ought to have been commended of you: for in nothing am I behind the very chiefest apostles, though I be nothing. 12 Truly the signs

of an apostle were wrought among you in all patience, in signs, and wonders, and mighty deeds.

Grace is the power of God at work in the lives of every child of God to do that which is impossible to do. It is the power at work for sanctification and the work of the kingdom. What you may not naturally be able to do, grace comes up to help you do. Grace is your qualification where you lack natural ability to perform. Where grace is absent, disgrace is present. The gateway out of disgrace in life is the grace of God. You cannot shun fornication, masturbation, pornographic viewing without the attached grace of God with you. You cannot succeed more than the grace that is available for you empowers. God's response at Christ's expense is what we call grace. When Jesus is at the front of your life, your ability is tied to His expense for you to perform. Let your cry beginning from now be, Lord, engrace me to be able to win every war of life. You are only engraced when you embrace God's grace for a tension free life. You shall no longer suffer any form of disgrace in Jesus name.

Grace is merited favour at the expense of Christ. Its greatest expression came in the gift of the life, death, and resurrection of Jesus on our behalf, something we could never earn or deserve without the intervention of heaven.

6. Be a Teen of Compassion.
Psalms 112:4
4 Unto the upright there ariseth light in the darkness: [he is] gracious, and full of compassion, and righteous

Compassion is what helps you to enjoy the passion of Christ for all-round rest. Compassion is what positions you for tension free life. No compassion, no compensation. Jesus was a man who was always moved with compassion, no wonder He enjoyed unlimited amounts of heavens compensation for His action with signs and wonders following in His ministry. By compassion you can do a mighty work that will open the windows of heavens for favour upon your life in all phases of your life.

Compassion is what pushes you to release yourself as a living sacrifice, holy, acceptable for the Master's use. This is the greatest commitment of man with greatest rewards. You can't have compassion for the sick and fall sick. You cannot have compassion for the poor and become poor. Your compassion for the 'failures' is what guarantees your success. Rise up and be compassionate, solving problems so that you can be free from them. Jesus was a friend to the friendless. He was sympathetic, kind and merciful. Do the same so that you can enjoy the throne with Him

7. Be a Teen of Humility
1 Peter 5:5 KJV
5 Likewise, ye younger, submit yourselves unto the elder. Yea, all of you be subject one to another, and be clothed with humility: for God resisteth the proud, and giveth grace to the humble.

Don't ever believe that your talents, gifts, abilities, successes and achievements come from you. If anyone deserves a pat on the back for those things, it's not you. Don't ever allow yourself to be full of self-centered pride. Don't ever be puffed up by a false sense of your own importance. Your parent's wealth is not your own, do not let that fill your head and consequently start misbehaving. Pride is a killer of destiny. You are not in any way better than anybody else, it is the grace of God that placed you where you see yourself. Be humble and respectful. Never allow any achievement to make you feel as if you are the achiever. God gave you everything you have at hand and it is not by your effort. Humility pays, it promotes, it dignifies and brings you to honour.

8. Be a Teen of Self-Control.
1 Peter 5:8 KJV
8 Be sober, be vigilant; because your adversary the devil, as a roaring lion, walketh about, seeking whom he may devour:

Rein yourself in and don't let the world set the agenda for how you live. The world will tell you how to live out your sexuality. The world will tell you how to view material things. The world will tell you how to treat other people. Sadly, the world will tell you that in these and all other areas you have the freedom to choose and use your own rules. But instead of living a life of excess, imitate Christ and live a life of discipline by striving to please God in these and all other areas.

9. Be a Teen of Respect and Obedience for Authority.
1 Samuel 2:30 KJV

30 Wherefore the LORD God of Israel saith, I said indeed [that] thy house, and the house of thy father, should walk before me for ever: but now the LORD saith, Be it far from me; for them that honour me I will honour, and they that despise me shall be lightly esteemed.

God is your King. He has established authorities in your life who you are called to respect, honour, and obey as long as they don't require you to do something in opposition to God's will. Yes, I know I've always reminded you that children are to obey their parents, but in addition, start respecting, honouring, and obeying your teachers, your coaches and all others in authority over you.

10. Be a Teen of Sexual Purity.
Gal 5:19KJV
Now the deeds of the flesh are evident, which are: immorality, impurity, sensuality,

Sexual immorality is the work of the flesh. Live in the spirit to enjoy tension free life. Your parents may have been nagging and admonishing you on the danger of sexual immorality. Pastors always speak about this issue. What is it all about it? It is a common thing among the youth. "Why can't they just stop talking about this sex thing!" We cannot stop talking about it because we don't want you to be prevented from your glorious destiny by sin. Hopefully, this one counsel against sexual sin, is to allow God's will and design for you to be manifest in order for you to experience His incredible gift of sexuality in a world that makes a joke out of God's sexual plan. Don't buy the lies of the devil, that there are no rules. Stand firm on this because there will be opportunity for sexual immorality and compromise which will result in regret. Decide now to live what you know to be true, trust and believe that God has your best interest in mind and He wants you to experience the joy of sexual fulfilment in the context of your life-long marital commitment to one man, one woman. You will never regret it as your action because you shall lose any taste for sexual immorality in Jesus name.

11. Be a Teen of Modesty.
Deuteronomy 22:5 KJV
5 The woman shall not wear that which pertaineth unto a man, neither shall a man put on a woman's garment: for all that do so [are] abomination unto the LORD thy God

Let Christ be you model. Your life must pattern after that which is good and is the will of God. Make scripture your guide and Jesus your role model. We live in a society that has lost all respect for female modesty. Suddenly, men have lost all modesty also to the world. The world around you will encourage you to 'let it all hang out'. Please, work to carefully, deliberately, and consciously honour God through what you say, how you act, and what you wear. Remember that in God's eyes, the only eyes you need to please; modesty, chastity, honour and restraint are all virtues. Live a holy and decent life at all times. Do not wait for another time, you can start now.

12. Be a Teen of Full Dependence on God.

Psalm 121 KJV

1{A Song of degrees.} I will lift up mine eyes unto the hills, from whence cometh my help.2My help cometh from the LORD, which made heaven and earth.3He will not suffer thy foot to be moved: he that keepeth thee will not slumber.4Behold, he that keepeth Israel shall neither slumber nor sleep.5The LORD is thy keeper: the LORD is thy shade upon thy right hand.6The sun shall not smite thee by day, nor the moon by night.7The LORD shall preserve thee from all evil: he shall preserve thy soul.8The LORD shall preserve thy going out and thy coming in from this time forth, and even for evermore

David was a man that solely depended on God for everything. God was committed to everything about him, so much so that he lost not a single war that he fought, and he fought the most wars above any other king in Israel. The state of absolute dependence on God is what makes God to take the battle over from you and gives you victory in return. Your head is too small, don't allow it to kill you. Leave all results to God and you will become tension free. David enjoyed the help of God more than any king in Israel as communicated to us in Psalm 121. Solomon wrote these wise words: "*Trust in the Lord with all your heart and lean not on your own understanding; in all your ways acknowledge him, and he will make your paths straight.*" Proverbs 3:6-7.

There's nothing to be added to that.

Chapter 15

Avoidance of Self-Consciousness - Pathway to Freedom

Shyness is rooted in fear. Fear is a robber of destiny, it enslaves. It capitalises on many things as an excuse. Shyness is one on the main cohort of fear. Shyness, an irrational fear of speaking up and being humiliated or ignored. Why are some people so afraid of speaking out? In my mind the main causes are oversensitivity and insecurity. When you allow too much of self-consciousness you will relegate yourself to the back bench of life. Unfortunately, shyness is an enormous detriment to success. For people who experience this problem, it's important to understand the causes and work towards overcoming it. God has not given you the spirit of fear, but of love and sound mind. Don't allow Satan to corrupt your mind. Nobody is as good as you are because when God was done about creating you, He said you were very good, certified OK.

For naturally quiet people, the fear of speaking can arise from a few bad experiences, especially at an early age. When an adult reacts angrily or dismissively to an attempt at self-expression, it's natural to take it personally and shy away from future expression. Growing up, it took me a long time to realize how self-centered people really are. The way someone reacts to something you say usually has nothing to do with you–it's more likely a reflection of the mood they're in or a recent event in their life.

A key to overcoming shyness is recognizing these perceived slights for what they are–meaningless. When someone reacts to you negatively, don't take it personally. Imagine the other person's perspective. Is there something that may have put them in a bad mood? Are they trying to cover up their own inadequacy? Considering the perspective of the other person makes it easier to put their reaction in the proper context. It's also essential to enable you to let go of bad experiences. When you dwell on a bad experience, it grows into something much more frightening than reality. Don't do this to yourself! The more you think about a bad experience the more power you give it. Don't blame yourself. Think about something constructive. The more you can fill your mind with positive memories of speaking up the easier it gets.

Other People Are Not Better than You.
Another important step in overcoming shyness is realizing that other people are basically the same as you. Everyone is insecure and afraid of embarrassment. Other people usually aren't as smart as you think. If you have a question, chances are someone else is wondering about the same thing.

Don't let one or two bad experiences dictate your entire opinion of humanity. By and large, people are friendly and interested in connecting with others. They'll respond favourably to your attempts at communicating. In most cases, people will be thrilled that you took the initiative to break the ice.

Embrace Self Worth
The second cause of shyness is insecurity. If you don't think you have anything valuable to contribute, what's the point of risking embarrassment?

To get over this you need to recognize the merit of your own thoughts and the value they present to others. It's ironic that the people most inclined towards shyness are often the most thoughtful. To reach your potential, you need to share yourself with the world. Your brilliant insights don't hold any value until they've enlightened someone else.

The best way to get accustomed to sharing is practice. Force yourself to speak up, especially when you don't want to. Sit in the front of the room and make yourself visible. Understand that sharing your insights with people is doing them a favour. Once you get used to opening up, you'll notice how positively people react. This will build your self-confidence and faith in the goodwill of others.

Be a Contributor
Overcoming shyness isn't just something you should do for yourself; it's also part of being a contributing member of society. When you have a thought or idea that deserves to be heard and don't share it, you're not only

hurting yourself by keeping quiet, you're hurting the people around you. Other people need you. They need your intelligence and insight. They need your help to work through problems. By hiding behind shyness, you limit the help you can give to your friends, family members, and colleagues.

I heard of a college professor who used to make a big deal about overcoming shyness. He called it a, "silly, foolish habit," and said, "the sooner you can break it the better." Shyness doesn't benefit anyone. Saving yourself a little embarrassment doesn't amount to much in the long run. By overcoming shyness, you give yourself the chance to be recognized and promoted. By overcoming shyness, you create opportunities and open yourself up to forming meaningful relationships.

Chapter 16

Self-Motivation - Pathway to Exploits

1Sam 30:6
6 And David was greatly distressed; for the people spake of stoning him, because the soul of all the people was grieved, every man for his sons and for his daughters: but David encouraged himself in the LORD his God.

The state of being tension free is rooted in personal motivation and encouragement. Peer pressure can be avoided with personal motivation not to be like others but to be what God has created you to be. When you are self-motivated, you are deaf to the hearing of other people's comment. Staying motivated is a struggle, our drive is constantly assaulted by negative thoughts and anxiety about the future. Everyone faces doubt and depression. What separates the highly successful is the ability to keep moving forward believing that all things work together for good for them that love God.

There is no simple solution for a lack of motivation. Even after escaping it, the challenge reappears at the first sign of a little set back. The key is understanding your thoughts and how they drive your emotions. By learning how to nurture motivating thoughts, neutralize negative ones, and focus on the task at hand, you can pull yourself out of a slump before it gains momentum. Never think of anything that is not good but rather think about all that is good and motivational. This is God's recommendation for thriving motivation

Phil 4:8 KJV
8 Finally, brethren, whatsoever things are true, whatsoever things are honest, whatsoever things are just, whatsoever things are pure, whatsoever things are lovely, whatsoever things are of good report; if there be any virtue, and if there be any praise, think on these things. 9Those things, which ye have both learned, and received, and heard, and seen in me, do: and the God of peace shall be with you.

Reasons for Lack of Motivation
There are 3 primary reasons we lack motivation.
1. **Lack of confidence** – If you don't believe you can succeed, what's the point in trying? Be confident in your ability and you will succeed. When you lack confidence you are bound to be under tension as you continue to develop in life.
   Philippians *4:13 (NKJV) 13 I can do all things through Christ[a] who strengthens me.*
   You can do all things through Christ whom you have confidence in.
2. **Lack of focus** – If you don't know what you want, do you really want anything? Never mind opposition, press on to meet with the prize of your high calling.
3. **Lack of direction** – If you don't know what to do, how can you be motivated to do it. Strive to be a child of vision. Discover God's plan for your life and identify what you know how to do best without the help any body and go after it.

How to enhance Confidence and Self-Motivation

1. The first motivation-killer is a lack of confidence. When this happens to me, it's usually because I'm focusing entirely on what I want and neglecting what I already have. When you only think about what you want, your mind creates explanations for why you aren't getting it. This creates negative thoughts. Past failures, bad breaks, and personal weaknesses dominate your mind. You become jealous of your competitors and start making excuses for why you can't succeed. In this state, you tend to make a bad impression, assume the worst about others, and lose self-confidence.

The way to get out of this thought pattern is to focus on gratitude. Set aside time to focus on everything positive in your life. Make a mental list of your strengths, past successes, and current advantages. We tend to take our strengths for granted and dwell on our failures. By making an effort to feel grateful, you'll realize how competent and successful you already are. This will rejuvenate your confidence and get you motivated to build on your current success.

It might sound strange that repeating things you already know can improve your mind-set, but it's amazingly effective. The mind distorts reality to confirm what it wants to believe. The more negatively you think, the more examples your mind will discover to confirm that belief. When you truly believe that you deserve success, your mind will generate ways to achieve it. The best way to bring success to yourself is to genuinely desire to create value for the rest of the world.

2. The second motivation-killer is a lack of focus. How often do you focus on what you don't want, rather than on a concrete goal. We normally think in terms of fear. I'm afraid of being poor. I'm afraid no one will respect me. I'm afraid of being alone. The problem with this type of thinking is that fear alone isn't actionable but rather deadly. Instead of doing something about our fear, it feeds on itself and drains our motivation.

If you're caught up in fear based thinking, the first step is focusing that energy on a well-defined goal. By defining a goal, you automatically define a set of actions. If you have a fear of poverty, create a plan to increase your income. It could be going back to school, obtaining a higher paying job, or developing profitable business ideas based on serving people. The key is moving from an intangible desire to concrete, measurable steps.

By focusing your mind on a positive goal instead of an ambiguous fear, you put your brain to work. It instantly begins devising a plan for success. Instead of worrying about the future you start to do something about it. This is the first step in motivating yourself to take action. When you know what you want, you become motivated to take action.

Establish Direction for Your Living
The final piece in the motivational puzzle is direction. If focus means having an ultimate goal, direction is having

a day-to-day strategy to achieve it. A lack of direction kills motivation because without an obvious next action we succumb to procrastination. An example of this is a person who wants to have a popular blog, but who spends more time reading posts about blogging than actually writing articles.

The key to finding direction is identifying the activities that lead to success. For every goal, there are activities that pay off and those that don't. Make a list of all your activities and arrange them based on results. Then make an action plan that focuses on the activities that lead to success.

Chapter 17

Commitment to Studying - Pathway to Tension Free Academics and Successful Adulthood

2 Timothy 2:15
15 Study to shew thyself approved unto God, a workman that needeth not to be ashamed, rightly dividing the word of truth.

There are two types of compulsory exams you have to write. The exams that come expectedly and those that are unexpected. There are scheduled and non-scheduled exams. Life exams are unplanned for, unexpected, and you cannot predict from where they come nor the duration of them. The known, scheduled and from familiar sources are also to be "written".

What makes them exams is the fact that you are expected to produce the result. The quality of the result however, will determine the level of the approval. You either pass or fail. You need extreme levels of preparation for extremely favourable results for the highest approval. Whether you are about to take final exams, Continuous Assessment, midterms, certification, accreditation or real life exams, you have to study hard to be able to pass any of the afore-mentioned. What you study stays. What you never study is never steady. Facing any exams could be stressful when you lack adequate preparations. Don't let the stress of writing an exam become a stress to you. Here are nine sure- fire ways to ensure you are ready physically, emotionally, intellectually, and spiritually to take those exams.

1. Pathway of Pray
Philippians 4: 6 KJV
6 - Be careful for nothing; but in every thing by prayer and supplication with thanksgiving let your requests be made known unto God.

You have the obligation to pray for your success to come. Nothing happens without prayer. The best solution to tension free academics is prayer. It is a demand from God for your success. When you pray you are asking, when you are thanking, you acknowledge. You need both to commit God for your academic success.

Before any study session spend a few moments praying. Sometimes teens think that God is only in the most spiritual parts of their lives, but God is in every aspect of your life. He wants you to succeed. Praying can bring you closer to God and make you feel a little stronger and relaxed going into test time.

2. Pathway of Fasting
Fasting is abstinence from food and every other pleasure. Most times, the fasting you need to do may be a fast off your computer game, or staying away from your telephone for one week, or doing away with internet for

one month or probably keep off from one particular friend for a while.

In your fast you gain spiritual command to decree what you want in your exams. It is not just enough to attend classes, write notes, attempt tests and sit for the final exams. There are brilliant people who are failures in exams. Satan does not want you to succeed because he wants to put you under pressure in life. Satan's intention is to give you tension until you are tired and give up your glorious destiny.

Daniel, a good example of exploits in the Bible fasted. No wonder he excelled in all competitions. He was a man of deeper understanding of the present and future through his commitment to prayer and fasting.

Prov 10:2-3 KJV
1In the third year of Cyrus king of Persia a thing was revealed unto Daniel, whose name was called Belteshazzar; and the thing was true, but the time appointed was long: and he understood the thing, and had understanding of the vision.2 In those days I Daniel was mourning three full weeks.3I ate no pleasant bread, neither came flesh nor wine in my mouth, neither did I anoint myself at all, till three whole weeks were fulfilled.

In fasting you conquer your exam challenges in the spirit realms. God reveals to you the secret things about your exams and life issues when you fast. Fasting is a spiritual means to fast track your destiny. What becomes of others who experience academic challenges is not your experience because of your equipping through your spiritual discipline. Do you want to live without tension at all times? Always schedule time to fast and pray about what you want your future to be. There lies in prayer and fasting your glorious future because God reveals it to you gradually as you keep fasting and praying.

Hear what God said concerning your future as you seek Him in fasting and prayer;
Jer 29 11-13 KJV
11For I know the thoughts that I think toward you, saith the LORD, thoughts of peace, and not of evil, to give you an expected end. 12Then shall ye call upon me, and ye shall go and pray unto me, and I will hearken unto you. 13And ye shall seek me, and find me, when ye shall search for me with all your heart.

Your glorious, tension free Teenage is guaranteed because of your fasting and prayer. Your destiny shall not be obscured in Jesus name.

3. Pathway of Quick Action

There is time for everything including the time to study. It is time for wise study action that guarantees success in all exams. Do not postpone till tomorrow what you can do in the now. Procrastination is the thief of time, so the wise say. The remaining hours you have left every day without doing what you could do is lost to the enemy, Satan. It can be easy to put off studying until the last minute but it will be too tedious. That will amount to studying with tension. The things going on around you can be tempting ways to procrastinate but don't give in to such demands, go ahead with your study with the mind-set that there are other times to do the other things rather than using the needed study time for the exams you have before you. Some teens also find excuses to fail, because they just give up learning. Exams are overwhelming and challenging. They are designed to test your academic limits, but you can learn to exceed the limits. You need to keep your pace reasonable and learn what you can. If you feel truly overwhelmed, discuss it with your teachers, parents, friends, or leaders. Sometimes they can help. Relate with people of like mind to confirm what you already know. You cannot succeed more than you relate. Relate with others of a like mind, the same way you relate with God.

4. Pathway of Studying Networking
Prov 27:17-18 KJV
17Iron sharpeneth iron; so a man sharpeneth the countenance of his friend.18Whoso keepeth the fig tree shall eat the fruit thereof: so he that waiteth on his master shall be honoured.

You need people around you but not just anybody. You need people who are more experienced than you in your pursuit. There are people that you need in your life to get what you want to achieve. There are people more brilliant than you and you know them. They could be your friends or older persons. There is the need for you to connect with them for you to pass in your exams. Create for yourself a study network, network yourself for success. You are either studying with people in your church youth circle, group or people in your school.

Having a study group can be very supportive and helpful. Your study group can take turns quizzing each other on different related courses. You can provide intellectual insight in certain areas on different subjects for one another. Sometimes you can just laugh and pray together to ease yourselves of exam tension when the pressure gets to be too much. Just be sure your study group is actually focused on studying and not jesting about unnecessary issues that have no value to be added to your academic life. Study with friends and combinations of groups that have what you need. You will end up becoming like them, sharing the same honour accorded successful people. You shall make it in Jesus name.

5. Pathway of Upfront Planning
Prov 20: 17-18 KJV
17Bread of deceit is sweet to a man; but afterwards his mouth shall be filled with gravel.18Every purpose is established by counsel: and with good advice make war.

Your wise planning is what will give you results that are desirable to you. If you do not plan on how to pass, you are planning on how to fail. If you do not have a particular success plan you cannot pass in any exam. Success is not accidental, it is a product of wise planning. You know that certain tests are coming up at the end of a particular course, so plan your study time wisely. You are expecting your graduation from school, you also have to expect that at final exam time, you will have a lot of tests within the span of a week or two, you should also have a plan of attack to win in your exams. Which areas will need more of your time? For many for example, mathematics is somehow difficult for them, plans to give it more attention must be made. You should by reason of good planning know which test comes first and which one comes next. Which subjects need review.

Your teachers should be giving you some guidance as to what will be on the exam, but you can also use your notes to guide you. Try and write down a study schedule so you know what you need to study and when you need to study it. Be sensitive to your spirit for divine guidance that will place you above others who have no God like you have. Your sensitivity will reduce your tension because you will be guided to what you need to concentrate on while others are busy studying what becomes irrelevant to you as revealed by the spirit of God. This is why you must be a spirit filled believer, born again, evidenced by speaking in tongues. You shall not be under from now on, you shall be above in Jesus name. You have the heritage of success but you have the responsibility to study.

6. Pathway of Balanced Diet
Psalms 103:5(KJV)
Who satisfieth thy mouth with good things; so that thy youth is renewed like the eagle's.

Teens are known for eating badly. They are drawn to junk food like chips, pies, donuts, crackers and cookies. However, you may find that those foods are not very helpful to your study habits. Foods high in sugar content may give you energy at first, but then your energy diminishes quickly. Try to eat healthy "brain foods" high in protein like nuts, fruit, and fish. If you really need a boost of energy, try a diet soda or sugar free energy drinks, but the best is to keep hydrated by drinking plenty of water. Eating well is living well. If you are not healthy, you cannot study hard to pass. Eating good food is imperative to your learning and development. Your youth is renewed as an eagle when you feed on good foods not junk food. Remember this if you are too selective, all healthy foods are good for you, even if you don't like the way they look or smell, just eat them and you will be nourished.

7. Pathway of Adequate Rest

Psalm 127(KJV)
127 Except the Lord build the house, they labour in vain that build it: except the Lord keep the city, the watchman waketh but in vain. 2 It is vain for you to rise up early, to sit up late, to eat the bread of sorrows: for so he giveth his beloved sleep

There was a common saying that says if you do not rest, you may be laid to rest. That is not your portion in Jesus name. You need to have a scheduled resting time no matter how tight your study schedule may be to make it to the end. One of the ways to rest is by having good sleep. Sleep is one of the most important tools you have in studying for exams. You may feel stressed and like you don't know everything you need to know, but a good night's sleep can help relieve that stress. A lack of sleep can end up clouding your judgement or increase your number of mistakes. Get at least 6 to 8 hours of sleep a night, including the night before your exam.

8. Pathway of Having Fun.

Even when it seems you are not assimilating anything from your study, just create some fun to liven up your life and free yourself from tension. Yes, exam time is stressful, and you may feel like you have to devote all your time to studying. Do not be afraid of having reasonable fun. However, if you develop a good plan you should have some time to spend with friends and family. Make some time to do some things with your youth group in your church or any other youth forum or platform that week, to just blow off steam or tension. Taking an hour or two to get away from the stress is a good thing. It will make your head a bit clearer when you are back to studying and you will feel re-energized and recharged for success. You need some fun before your exams to have fun at the end of your exams.

9. Pathway of Self Examination.

1 Kings 18:41-19:8 (NLT)

41 Then Elijah said to Ahab, "Go get something to eat and drink, for I hear a mighty rainstorm coming!"

42 So Ahab went to eat and drink. But Elijah climbed to the top of Mount Carmel and bowed low to the ground and prayed with his face between his knees. 43 Then he said to his servant, "Go and look out toward the sea." The servant went and looked, then returned to Elijah and said, "I didn't see anything." Seven times Elijah told him to go and look. 44 Finally the seventh time, his servant told him, "I saw a little cloud about the size of a man's hand rising from the sea." Then Elijah shouted, "Hurry to Ahab and tell him, 'Climb into your chariot and go back home. If you don't hurry, the rain will stop you!'"45 And soon the sky was black with clouds. A heavy wind brought a terrific rainstorm, and Ahab left quickly for Jezreel. 46 Then the Lord gave special strength to Elijah. He tucked his cloak into his belt[a] and ran ahead of Ahab's chariot all the way to the entrance of Jezreel.

Elijah had an assignment from God to turn the heart of men from other gods to the Almighty God. For him to accomplish the task, he had to write an exam of praying a rain down on King Ahab's request. He started praying but nothing like rain came into view, he prayed severally and kept asking his servant to check for rain. This is self-examination. He kept praying and he kept checking. Until you see the expected result you desire, you have to keep studying and examining yourself if you have gotten it right to pass in an exam using Elijah's concept.

You need self-practice and self-examination of your level of assimilation to succeed to the end. How do you perform self-examination? Do self-practice or work through of your courses, prepare your examination using the standard examination guidelines and follow it, such as timing. Write your own examination. Mark your own examination and score yourself. Be sincere about the outcome and reattempt again and again until you can confidently confirm your high proficiency of understanding. This is what has worked for me in all my study matters and examinations including professional exams.

Studying in advance is what guarantees your advantage in the exams. You need strategic studying approaches to succeed in exams. As you are studying, take some note cards and write down questions that you think may be relevant in an exam. Then compile your note cards and begin answering your questions. If you get it wrong, just look up the answer. By taking the practice test you will be much more prepared for the real thing and you are sure to successfully complete your exam. You are destined to succeed anytime, anywhere. All you need is adequate preparation with a winning strategy.

10. Pathway of Relaxation

One great way to succeed in every exams is to be very relaxed. When you are not relaxed you are tensed. When you are under tension you have lost attention to details. The examiners know that there is tension to sit for an exam, which is why they also control your anxiety by giving you instructions such as do not start until you are told to do so. You even must plan to take a break. Breaks are a good thing when studying is becoming tensed. Studying can also be stressful on you a times. Step away from what you are studying and just clear your head with something different. It will help make you feel fresh to continue with fresh energy and a refined mind.

To relax is not to be slack but to be strengthened and refreshed. The following are avenues for productive relaxation.

1. **Listen** to inspirational music, preferably Gospel music that can illuminate you and re-ignite you into a sound intellectual realm.

2. **Watching** Gospel films, or humorous videos that have sound moral content and challenge you to be a better Christian as well as stimulate your laughter; laughing releases tension and enables you to feel refreshed.

3. **Discussion** and Cross-examination of subject matter of the exam with a course mate and friend. With this method, you are studying without tension. It is the process of rubbing minds with the right person on your course of study. This is why you need to choose your friends carefully. If your friend is not helping you out on your study concern, you will soon be a concern.

   If you are a friend of an empty-headed person, your head will soon be empty because you will become common being such a person's friend. You need a friend that has what you need and you will begin to have uncommon results.

Chapter 18

Understanding the A-Z of Life's Demands - Pathway for Teenager's Effectiveness into Adulthood

- ➤ A: Acquire a Strong and Positive Attitude
- ➤ B: Break Out of Your Shell; you need yourself to be what you are called to be.
- ➤ C: Characterize Your Hero after Christ
- ➤ D: Demand Respect for Your Standards, Yourself and Your Beliefs, never allow any intimidation.
- ➤ E: Energize Yourself Every day With a Goal of Making a Difference, and pursue it
- ➤ F: Failure to Plan, is Planning for Failure; without you knowing, in ignorance.
- ➤ G: Go for God to get the Gold; Go Big or Go Home without any gold.
- ➤ H: Humility is the price for God to embrace you with favour.
- ➤ I: Itemize Your Qualities and See your Strengths Not Your Weaknesses
- ➤ J: Jealousy Will Always influence you the Negatively Not Positively.
- ➤ K: Keep your Momentum, Never Stop, and Keep Moving until you win!
- ➤ L: Live Your Life and never allow any distraction
- ➤ M: Magnify Your Opportunities, make use of them to the attraction of others.

- ➤ N: Nothing is better than the Truth, you fly with it.
- ➤ O: Only the faithful can be fruitful, pursue after it.
- ➤ P: Position Yourself in Positive Environments, seek positive impart.
- ➤ Q: Quality Over Quantity is a mark of distinction
- ➤ R: Realize Problems and Quickly Fix Them, never wait to watch issues.
- ➤ S: Stick to the Purpose and stay focused,
- ➤ T: Treasure All Your Godly Friends, For They're Your Most Prized Possessions that you have.
- ➤ U: Understand That All Things Have a Purpose and time to fulfil them.
- ➤ V: Visualize Success and Don't Be Afraid of taking steps. You Miss 100% of The Steps You Don't Take.
- ➤ W: Work Hard If You Expect Success and sweetness.
- ➤ X: X-ray your steps with the Word to know if they are ordered by God.
- ➤ Y: Yes, is Not Always the Answer. Learn to Say No, just be yourself acting on God's instructions.
- ➤ Z: Zoom into Revelation, and Zip the Revolution

Chapter 19

Understanding A-Z Acronyms of Life Experiences - Pathway to Tension Free Teenage

> ➢ Attitude is the price for altitude
> ➢ Be careful of bad friends, it is the way to tension free life.
> ➢ Continually give thanks throughout your Teenage
> ➢ Do not ever blame others for your shortcomings, stay responsible.
> ➢ Even when the times are hard you are exempted by covenant with God.
> ➢ Following after God makes you a leader of the people.
> ➢ God is forever able to do all things
> ➢ Hold on to your faith in God
> ➢ Inspiration from God is the gateway for intelligence required foe exploit
> ➢ Joy of the Lord is your strength
> ➢ Keep thanking Him for all the things He has done for you.
> ➢ Love of God is a surety for tension free Teenage
> ➢ Mind the word and the world will mind you.
> ➢ No weapon that is formed against you will prevail
> ➢ Only Jesus guarantees justice and safety
> ➢ Praise and press to meet up with your expectations.
> ➢ Quit looking at the past, it could harmful to your future

➢ **R**edeem your time, make use of your now to make your life count.
➢ **S**tart every day with thanksgiving
➢ **T**o "thank" is a command without alternative.
➢ **U**nveil your destiny, do not allow your potential to go stagnant
➢ **V**ision with precision is what makes life precious for living
➢ **W**inning is not luck, it is the reward of your walking with God.
➢ **X**-ray your life with God's Word to avoid pitfalls in life.
➢ **Y**ou are a product of what you believe
➢ **Z**eal geared towards His kingdom is what makes a king out of you

Chapter 20

Wisdom - the Pathway to Teenage Maturity and Advancement

What makes us wise is the word. There is no idle word, every word you hear today is a seed planted for your tomorrow if it is not required by your immediate need. The more worded you are the weightier you become. What makes a heavy weight of man is the word; that is why the only thing your teachers do with you in your school is to stuff you with words on any particular subject. When you pay attention, you have escaped the tension of failure. The word of God is superior and weightier than any other words. The word of God is anything you are thinking of. Are you thinking of a solution to a problem, are you thinking about inventions, innovations, success, good health, good friends, high grades in the school etc.? The word of God is what you need to create and recreate your world. Selected words of wisdom for teenage guidance lead to tension free adulthood.

Solomon in his wisdom, collected the sayings of the world and then compared them with the Word of God in the book of Ecclesiastes. I believe that was what made Solomon the wisest king to ever have lived. No wonder he ruled without tension. It is important in our life to be able to distinguish what is from the world and what is from God. The Word of God is your guide for living an effective and tension free life. The word of the Word is eternal information to avoid deformation. Many a time, you may receive wise counsel from others, but it is never absolute, therefore, you need to consult with God through His word. The ability to distinguish between the two makes one wise and makes the journey one with less stress and tension free.

Chapter 21

Some Selected God's Word Counsel

The following quotes are Bible-based words of wisdom and caution for tension free Teenage. Read them and let them be your guide in your decision-making at every crossroad of your life.

➢ A gentle answer turns away wrath (Prov 15:1)
➢ Pride goes before destruction (Prov16:18)
➢ A good name is more desirable than great riches (Prov. 22:1)
➢ As iron sharpens iron so one man sharpens another (Prov 27:17)
➢ Saved by the skin of your teeth (Job 19:20)
➢ Do to others as you would have them do to you (Matt 7:12)
➢ It is not good that man should be alone (Gen 2:18)
➢ A land flowing with milk and honey (Ex 3:8)
➢ Man does not live by bread alone (Deut. 8:3)
➢ A still small voice (I Kings19:12)
➢ Two heads are better than one (Ecclesiastes 4:9)
➢ It takes two to agree (Amos 3:3)
➢ As he think in his heart, so is he (Prov 23:7)
➢ Whoever digs a hole will fall into it (Eccl 10:8)
➢ They have sown the wind and will reap the whirlwind (Hosea 8:7)
➢ Where your treasure is, there your heart will be also (Matt 6:21)
➢ No man can serve two masters (Matt 6:24)

- ➤ A wolf in sheep's clothing (Matt 7:15)
- ➤ A pearl of great price (Matt 13:46)
- ➤ The blind leading the blind (Matt 15:14)
- ➤ Seek and you will find (Matt 7:7)
- ➤ A city set on a hill cannot be hidden. (Matt 5:14)
- ➤ He who keeps his mouth keeps his life (Prov 13:3)
- ➤ Don't cast your pearls before swine. (Matt 7:6)
- ➤ What is good for the goose, is good for the gander.

Chapter 22

Some Selected Words from Great Minds in the World

The following words are words of caution and counsels from the great minds in the world. These are not biblical words but many of them have some elements of light that could also encourage you. They are powerful words but when you compare them with the Word of God, you will find God's word to be the most powerful. The intensity of 'God's Word light' cannot be compared with the word of wisdom of men.

➢ Children should be seen and not heard.
➢ He who fell into the pit sends wise caution to the on comers to avoid falling into it.
➢ Too big for your britches.
➢ Sticks and stones may break my bones, but words will never hurt me.
➢ Too cold for comfort.
➢ If you play with fire you will get burnt.
➢ Better safe than sorry.
➢ Innocent until proven guilty.
➢ You can lead a horse to water but you can't make him drink.
➢ He who hesitates is lost.
➢ You are what you eat.
➢ Beauty is only skin deep.
➢ Necessity is the mother of invention.
➢ A friend in need is a friend indeed.
➢ A rolling stone gathers no moss.

- Oil and water don't mix.
- A stitch in time saves nine.
- A watched pot never boils.
- If at first you don't succeed, try, try, again.
- The squeaky wheel gets the grease.
- A bird in hand is worth two in the bush.
- Silence is golden.
- You can't judge a book, by its cover page the inside may be stinking.
- Don't count your chickens before they hatch.
- Cleanliness is next to godliness.
- Where there's smoke, there's fire.
- Don't cry over spilled milk.
- People who live in glass houses don't throw stones.
- The early bird gets the worm.
- An apple a day, keeps you away from the doctor.
- All's fair in love and war.
- Look before you leap.
- All work and no play makes Jack a dull boy.

Chapter 23

The Winning Word for Easy Passage to Adulthood

- ➢ Winning may not be everything, but losing is nothing compared to winning.
- ➢ You cannot stand tall without standing on someone.
- ➢ You can be a victor without having victims.
- ➢ If I am not worth the game, I am surely not worth the winner.
- ➢ When you are at all times on the right side you can win at all times without ever losing.
- ➢ Take up a challenge big enough to matter, small enough to win.
- ➢ You matter only when you mind the one that matters because He is the matter that matters to be minded.
- ➢ If you must be at the center, you must make Him to be at the center or you will never be near the center.
- ➢ You're not under duress to win. But you are compelled to keep trying to do the best you can every day.
- ➢ Conquer, but don't triumph, you dominate by conquering.
- ➢ Greatness is not in where you stand, but in the direction you are moving.
- ➢ We sometimes sail in the direction of the wind and sometimes against it, but you must sail either way and not drift, nor stop at anchor.
- ➢ It is not honourable to triumph by trickery, you triumph with integrity.

- ➢ Sin always look shining from the distance, when approach with prayer you see how ugly it is.
- ➢ Your own way may look very good but when you consider God's way, you see how excellent His way is.
- ➢ Do not think too much of yourself during your teens if you don't want tension, rely responsibly on you dependants.
- ➢ Never say never because you may never have the opportunity to ever make the second chance if you say never.

Chapter 24

Wise Counsels - Pathway to Wisdom and Long Life

Jesus Christ is our perfect example and standard with which to measure our character and personal growth and development, He also offers some guidelines which will help all of us mould our characters into what our God would have them to be. You cannot know unless you are told. Wise counsel is the bases for wise living and long life. According to His counsel, there are vital attributes that you need to possess for tension free living. The following are Godly counsel for your tension free passage from teen to adult.

1. Be born again. A born again is a Christian who wears the name of the Lord as the breastplate of salvation. It shows he belongs to Jesus and that he is living in accordance with His will. Do not claim to be a Christian if you are not willing to conform your life, your thoughts and actions to the doctrine of Christ (2 John 9).This is why you have to accept Him(Jesus) as your Lord and Saviour and confess Him as so with your mouth from your heart. If you are not saved you are not safe. Until you give your life to Christ, you are prone to tension.

John 3:2-3 KJV
2this man came to Jesus by night and said to Him, "Rabbi, we know that You have come from God as a teacher; for no one can do these signs that You do unless

God is with him." 3Jesus answered and said to him, "Truly, truly, I say to you, unless one is born again he cannot see the kingdom of God."

2. Be filled with the Holy Spirit.

3. Learn self-discipline.
Learn to say no to self, friends, evil ways, bad habits, etc. Jesus taught self-denial (Matt. 16:24). The apostle Peter taught that self-control is to be added to our faith (2 Pet. 1:5-7). A lack of self-discipline is one sure sign of immaturity and that can lead to tension- filled living even after maturity. You are bound to make the biggest mistakes if you are not self-disciplined and that can affect the circle of your existence in life.

4. Be unselfish.
Selfishness, the seat of all sins and wrongdoing, is having too much concern with one's own welfare. It was evidently described in Scripture by both Lot (Gen. 13:8-13) and the rich fool (Luke 12:16-20). It is impossible to make a right decision and be selfish. Moses, in choosing to lead the children of Israel, acted selflessly (Heb. 11:24-26) while on the other hand, Lot, acting in a purely selfish manner, made a terrible choice which led to tragic consequences. (Gen. 13:8). Someone has suggested that a golden rule to follow is 'God first, others, second and self, third.'

5. Good judgement.
Be able to see the difference between good and evil, between right and wrong . Judge a thing not only by

what it is but also by what it will eventually lead to if it is followed to its end, such as social drinking, smoking and unholy partying. Additionally, do not choose for the present but the future because your future needs more attention than your now. The patriarch Lot chose for the present while Moses chose for the future.

6. Develop strong convictions.
Develop strong scriptural beliefs on all important issues. No one respects a person who is "unstable in all his ways." Stand with your convictions even if you must stand alone. Consider the Apostle Paul (2 Tim. 4:16) and Jesus (Mark 14:50). Do not be afraid to express your conviction. Consider how the prophet Daniel boldly stated his convictions while a captive in Babylon

Dan. 1:1-21 NKJV
8 But Daniel purposed in his heart that he would not defile himself with the portion of the king's delicacies, nor with the wine which he drank; therefore he requested of the chief of the eunuchs that he might not defile himself. 9 Now God had brought Daniel into the favor and goodwill of the chief of the eunuchs. 10 And the chief of the eunuchs said to Daniel, "I fear my lord the king, who has appointed your food and drink. For why should he see your faces looking worse than the young men who are your age? Then you would endanger my head before the king." 11 So Daniel said to the steward whom the chief of the eunuchs had set over Daniel, Hananiah, Mishael, and Azariah, 12 "Please test your servants for ten days, and let them give us vegetables to eat and water to drink. 13 Then let our appearance be examined before you, and the appearance of the young

men who eat the portion of the king's delicacies; and as you see fit, so deal with your servants." 14 So he consented with them in this matter, and tested them ten days.15 And at the end of ten days their features appeared better and fatter in flesh than all the young men who ate the portion of the king's delicacies. 16 Thus the steward took away their portion of delicacies and the wine that they were to drink, and gave them vegetables.17 As for these four young men, God gave them knowledge and skill in all literature and wisdom; and Daniel had understanding in all visions and dreams. 18 Now at the end of the days, when the king had said that they should be brought in, the chief of the eunuchs brought them in before Nebuchadnezzar. 19 Then the king interviewed them, and among them all none was found like Daniel, Hananiah, Mishael, and Azariah; therefore they served before the king. 20 And in all matters of wisdom and understanding about which the king examined them, he found them ten times better than all the magicians and astrologers who were in all his realm. 21 Thus Daniel continued until the first year of King Cyrus.

7. Develop good habits.

A habit is a thing done often and hence, usually done easily. It is a practice, custom or act that is acquired and becomes automatic. There are two kinds of habits good and bad. Form good habits in life and abstain from the bad ones.

Be and Do Your Best. '*Whatever your hand finds to do, do it with your might*' *Eccl. 9:10*. Consider Joseph, he always did his best whether he found himself as a slave, prisoner or governor.

8. Be independent.

Think for yourself. Do not be a slave to another's thinking, especially when it has to do with your beliefs. Do not let anybody sell you out to unholy beliefs. Be the one that brings them to the obedience of your God. Thinking correctly has many benefits as outlined in Proverbs 23:7: *"For as he thinks in his heart, so is he."* Therefore, manage the way you think. *"Bring every thought in captivity to the obedience of Christ"* 2 Cor. 10:5, Phil. 4:8.Never must you think failure nor sickness nor diseases. Never think about anything unholy, not masturbation, not lusting about anything in your thoughts.

9. Do not use vulgar language or corrupt words. *"Let your speech always be with grace, seasoned with salt, that you may know how you ought to answer each one"* Col. 4:6. Never compromise your words; you will never consider it as an alternative. Do not be conformed to what others are saying but to what God is saying. Learn how to communicate with the Word. When others are saying "they are dead" be saying "you shall not die but live". A lack of the word of God in communication causes many tensions and allows tension to wait for you in the future. Always express yourself with scripture, you don't need to say the Book, Chapter and verses in most occasions, just communicate scripturally. Do not use filthy or profane language like those of the world you are in (Eph. 4:29). Profanity is scorned by all right-thinking people. In reality, it is a sign of stupidity. The tongue may be hard to control (Jas. 3:1-12), but it can be and must be controlled.

10. Be of Good Behaviour.

'Be an example to the believers and non- believers in word, in conduct, in love, in spirit, in faith, in purity,' 1 *Tim. 4:12.*

This exhortation was particularly targeted at the teenagers and youth by Apostle Paul who was instructing Timothy to conduct himself properly so that no one would "despise his youth." Young people need to behave properly in the home by respecting their parents (Eph. 6:1), in the school by respecting the rules and teachers, and in public by conforming to established rules and guiding principles. Those who are older need to set the example for the younger and be consistent with the display of such virtues, not requiring from young people what they do not require of themselves. A good rule for all when it comes to behaviour is to not do anything you would not want to be doing when Jesus comes. Do not do anything in your private life that you would not be comfortable doing when people are there with you.

11. Be a 'Teen' of precision.

Be definite in aim and purpose. God created everything for a definite purpose, especially you. Be purposeful in living. Do not drift through life just taking it as it comes. Have an aim in life. Establish proper goals and work hard to reach them. Be determined but not stubborn. Of course, as a Christian, your life is filled with purpose. The Word of God admonishes you,

"Let us hear the conclusion of the whole matter: fear God and keep His commandments, for this is man's all.

For God will bring every work into judgment, including every secret thing, whether good or evil", Eccl. 12:13-14.

Never forget that your ultimate goal is heaven. That will help you to be precise about your mission, keep focused in living each day in the proper manner.

12. Responsible to your family.

Whatever your situation in relation to your natural family, do what you can to make it what God would have it to be. Be totally submissive and responsible to your home's ethics and guiding principles. Until you are fully equipped for life, never walk out on your family. You are a child still living at home with your parents, conduct yourself respectfully. Obey their rules, listen to their advice, seek their guidance. As you progress and advance in age, if you are contemplating marriage, choose a companion who not only loves you but above all, loves God. When becoming someone's spouse, apply the teachings of Scripture to your relationship. *Husbands, love your wives*(Eph. 5:25). *Wives, be subject unto your husbands*, (Eph. 5:22) *and love them*,(Titus 2:4).Do not in any way modernize your marriage more than the scriptural expectation. When you become a parent, *bring up your children in the nurture and admonition of the Lord* (Eph. 6:4) as you were by your parents. Often, happiness in this life and the eternal destiny of one's soul in the life to come is in large part determined by relationships in the physical family. Your true character is tested by how you act and react toward family. This is why the emphasis on being responsible in your home as a Teen is vital. That is the sure assurance that you are following the golden path to become a responsible adult.

In conclusion!

Ecc 12:13 Let us hear the conclusion of the whole matter: Fear God, and keep his commandments: for this is the whole duty of man.

Every pathways you have gone through in this book and other vital counsels are God's instructions for you greater tomorrow. By strength shall no man prevail. You cannot transcend until you are transformed. Transformation comes by the information you have and processed into useful product. The word of God is the only true raw material for transformation. When the word of God comes, it revealed and that becomes revelation. However, the guarantee for transformation is the word that is revealed to you, you are convinced by the word and you take a step to ensure that you are converted to the true nature of the word. You have hard that the only way to transit without tension into adulthood and maintain the tempo of rest as an adult is by the word. If you are not born again, you will only stop at information reading this book. If you need transformation, you need revelation. God only reveals to His Children.

Romans 8:14
[14] For as many as are led by the Spirit of God, they are the sons of God.

115

Therefore, you need to be born-again to become a child of God with access to revelation for tension free graduation into adult and become a perfect adult, without future unrest in every areas of your life. Remember a tension free Teenage leads to a responsible adulthood. But the process of transformation between teenage to adult is your identity with God.

Prayer of transformation.
Lord Jesus, I have decided to make a difference in life, walking through my teenage to adult without tension. I am a sinner. I hereby confess my sin to you today. Forgive me and let my name be written in the Book of life that I might serve you for the rest of my life.
Thank you for forgiven me. Now, I am born-again. I am now a believer. I have been transformed, tension free to become a responsible adult. Thank you Jesus.

Congratulations! You are now born-again. You are free from the teenage tension and transformed to become a responsible adult.

I hereby pray with you in the name of Jesus, every steps you take from today shall become an investment for your stress less adulthood in Jesus name. I decreed in the name of Jesus, you shall not have any regret in life. You shall scale through every hurdles of the teenahehood without hurt. You shall be among the responsible adult in your own time. You shall make it to the end, in Jesus name, amen.

BOOKS BY SAME AUTHOR

Coming Out Soon:

- ❖ Teen, Pathway To Adulthood.
- ❖ Christ Modelled Youth
- ❖ Heads Up For Mastery
- ❖ Youth Foundation

Still in the Process of Writing:

- ❖ I Got the Answers
- ❖ Parenting Revolution
- ❖ The Uncommon Youth
- ❖ Spice Up Your Youth with the Word
- ❖ The Mystery of the Firstborn
- ❖ Leading or Dealing (Leadership Disparity)
- ❖ Mind the Minor
- ❖ Heart-Look
- ❖ Parenting with Insight

WATCH OUT!

CPSIA information can be obtained at www.ICGtesting.com
Printed in the USA
LVOW08s0107230115

423969LV00009B/77/P